Five-Card Majors

This book provides an exciting challenge to all bridge players, whether they use four- or five-card major opening bid systems or base their game on Acol, Standard American, or any other system.

Ron Klinger, whose books have achieved international recognition for their clarity, provides an admirably lucid introduction to five-card majors and demonstrates the system's many virtues. Approximately two thirds of the world's leading bridge players use some system based on opening with five-card major suits.

The detailed analysis of the system and its applications in pairs play are backed up by carefully chosen exercises that will enable players to consolidate their grasp of five-card major methods. Moreover, the answers to the bidding problems are much more than bald solutions — they are accompanied by succinct explanations showing how the final contracts were reached.

If you want to put an edge on your game, you have to read *Five-Card Majors*!

Standard American Edition

FIVE-CARD
MAJORS

RON KLINGER

A Master Bridge Series title
in conjunction with Peter Crawley

Houghton Mifflin Company
Boston • New York • London

To Phillip

A remarkable friend

and a great source of inspiration

For information about permission to reproduce selections from
this book, write to Permissions, Houghton Mifflin Company,
215 Park Avenue South, New York, New York 10003.
The right of Ron Klinger to be identified as the author has been
asserted by him in accordance with the Copyright, Designs and
Patents Act of 1988.

Library of Congress Cataloging-in-Publication Data

Klinger, Ron. Five-card majors / Ron Klinger.
p.   cm.
"A Master bridge series title in conjunction with Peter Crawley."
Reprint. Previously published: London : V. Gollancz in association with
P. Crawley, 1992.
ISBN 0-395-62948-9
1. Contract bridge — Bidding.   I. Title. II. Title: Five-card majors.
III. Series: Master bridge series.
GV1282.4.K56   1992
795.41'52 — dc20   92-5480
CIP

Printed in the United States of America
BP 10 9 8 7 6 5 4 3 2 1

Contents

Introduction

There are many good bidding systems. For the most part it matters little which system you and your partner play. The real crux is how well you and partner know it and how competently you can use it.

Nevertheless, most players in the world play some system based on opening five-card majors. The vast majority of players in the United States plays five-card majors as does a significant number in Europe, Asia, Australia and New Zealand.

The majority of pairs competing at international level use systems based on five-card majors and the winners of World Championships almost invariably feature the five-card major structures.

This book is intended as an introduction to five-card major methods. The reader is assumed to have an understanding of how bridge is played as well as the rudiments of bidding strategy.

The book is divided into two parts. The first deals with Standard Methods which are most commonly used by those who play five-card majors. The second half contains popular methods which are generally found among duplicate devotees.

For the reader who plays Acol or some other system based on opening four-card suits, this will give you an inkling of how the other half lives. You may find parts that you will wish to adapt into your own methods. You may even find yourself trying out five-card majors to see how they work. A word of warning: Most who try five-card majors do not wish to revert to playing four-card suits.

For the reader who already plays five-card majors, the book provides a summary of the methods generally played. You may find parts which reinforce what you already do. You may find areas that are new to you and will enhance your game.

Each segment is liberally illustrated with quizzes and partnership bidding exercises. You are urged to tackle all of these exercises which complement the written instruction. Do well on the exercises and you will do well at the table, too.

Ron Klinger, 1992

Chapter 1

Why Five-Card Majors Are Better

It is not critical whether you play four-card majors or five-card majors (despite the blusterings of the fanatics of each approach). As long as you and your partner play the same system and know your system thoroughly, your results will not suffer in the long term from the fact that the system is based on four-card majors or five-card majors. You should play the system that suits your style, the system with which you feel comfortable.

If there were one clearly superior method, all the top players would adopt that approach. Of course! Yet what do we find? In any international championship, it is hard to find two pairs playing exactly the same system. It's not what you play but how you play that counts.

Nevertheless, an analysis of the systems played in world championships reveals that about 65% of the pairs play some system based on five-card majors and the rest play systems based on four-card suits or highly exotic methods. This does not prove that five-card majors are better and those who prefer five-card majors do not all play the same system. While the systems may vary, they do have in common that the One Heart and One Spade opening bids promise at least five cards in that suit.

This preference does show that the majority of experts favour some five-card major basis which they feel gives them sufficient benefits to continue with this system. All systems have the same underlying strategy, to locate an eight-card or better major suit fit. When your point count is in the 24–29 range, game in an eight-card major fit is more likely to succeed than 3NT and is also likely to outscore 3NT when both contracts succeed. Also a partscore in a major suit fit is more likely to come home than 1NT (or 2NT). Those who choose five-card majors believe that this approach is more efficient in locating the desired major suit fits regularly.

Playing five-card majors has one enormous advantage. It is a tension-reliever for your partnership, more powerful than Valium.

The tension-reducing elements when playing five-card major openings include:

- You do not need to rebid your suit to indicate a five-card holding.

If you open 1♡ or 1♠ and partner responds 1NT, you can pass or raise no-trumps without fearing that a 5–3 major fit has gone begging. This sort of problem besets those playing four-card suits. Suppose you pick up:

♠ AJ3
♡ KQ862
◇ A4
♣ J98

Playing a weak no-trump, you can open 1♡ and rebid 1NT over 1♠ to show your values. If playing four-card suits, a 5–3 heart fit could go begging here. Partner may well pass 1NT rather than put you into 2♡ with only three-card support.

Playing five-card majors, you can rest easy and rebid 1NT. If 2♡ is the right spot, partner has enough information to put you there. Playing four-card suits and a strong no-trump presents the same problem. Your rebid cannot convey your no-trump strength and the extra card in your major. To rebid in a three-card minor will confirm the five-card major but will distort your shape. Partner may even pass the minor suit rebid.

With five-card majors, the major suit length is solved with the opening bid and you can then bid the number of no-trumps your hand is worth. Partner then has all the relevant information to make a sensible decision.

Suppose you pick up:

♠ AK87
♡ K8743
◇ A2
♣ 52

You open 1♡ and partner responds 1NT. What now?

Playing five-card majors, you can pass knowing that no useful major suit fit exists and 1NT is likely to be the best partscore. Playing four-card suits, you would be anxious since a 5–3 major fit may yet exist. You should still pass 1NT – it would be unsound to rebid 2♡ – but you cannot shake off that nagging doubt.

- Responder is able to give a three-card raise to the two-level without fear of playing in a 4–3 fit.

- Where responder does not give support at once for a five-card major, delayed support may be made with just a doubleton.

If the bidding starts 1♠ : 1NT, 2◇ : 2♠, playing five-card majors, responder will generally hold just two spades. Opener will therefore not become too enthusiastic. Playing four-card suits, responder might have three-card support and, expecting an eight-card fit, opener might push too high.

- The 5–3 major fits are found on the first round of bidding. The 4–4 fits are located on the second round.

WEST	EAST	Opening 1♠ leads to the worst result :
♠ AQ54	♠ 82	1♠ : 1NT, Pass. Opening 1♡ allows
♡ Q762	♡ A985	1♡ : 2♡. Playing five-card majors,
◇ A7	◇ KJ4	1♣ : 1♡, 2♡, so that it takes one extra bid
♣ J43	♣ 9862	to find the best spot. Opening a weak 1NT

misses the heart contract entirely.

- Opening 1♣ or 1◇ on most hands allows you to gauge whether the opponents are strong enough to overcall.

One of the benefits of the weak no-trump and frequent openings of 1♠ and 1♡ (on four-card suits) is that the opposition may not be strong enough to venture an overcall at the two-level. However it may be of considerable benefit to know what strength is held by the opposition. Instead of fearing intervention, you should welcome it as it enables you to place the strength, the distribution and the requirements to counter it. 'Know thine enemy', is sound advice for any army and any bridge game, too.

Given that the partnership uses takeout doubles wholeheartedly at the one-level and two-level, there is nothing to fear from their overcalls. Indeed, enabling them to overcall may assist responder's bidding problems. In addition, if your side ends up as declarer, their overcall may assist you in the play of the hand. It is largely a matter of confidence in your own judgement. If you believe the opponents can judge the auction better than you, you should try to shut them out. If you believe your judgment is better than theirs, you will be happy to have them enter the auction.

- In a competitive auction, responder can support opener's major in comfort with only three trumps.

♠ KQ7
♡ Q43
♦ J10432
♣ J6

Partner opens 1♡ and right-hand opponent jumps to 3♣ (weak). Your action? You are too weak for 3♦ and, playing four-card suits, there is a fair degree of risk in bidding 3♡.

Playing five-card majors, you can bid 3♡ in sleep . . . no worries. You know that you are in an eight-card fit at least.

Playing four-card suits, partner on hearing 3♡ is also prone to an anxiety attack. If holding only four hearts, the questions continue. Is the raise to 3♡ genuine with four-card support? Is it a forced raise with only three trumps? Should I try 3NT rather than 4♡? And on it goes. Five-card majors reduce the worry level in competitive auctions and after pre-emptive overcalls.

- Playing four-card suits, most 4–4–3–2 and 4–3–3–3 hands are opened in a minor suit even when a major is available.

(a)   With four spades and four clubs, the standard opening is 1♣.
(b)   With four spades and four diamonds OR four hearts and four clubs, the standard opening is in the minor suit, allowing both suits to be shown at the one-level much of the time.
(c)   With a 4–3–3–3 pattern and a 4-card major, the opening is often 1♣. This gives partner room to bid at the one-level and allows a strong opening hand to rebid in no-trumps. Opening 1♡ or 1♠ often buys a 1NT response with the no-trumps contract now placed in an inferior position, with the weaker hand as declarer.

- Competitive bidding at the three-level works best when you know the number of trumps held by your side.

WEST	NORTH	EAST	SOUTH
1♠	2♦	2♠	3♦
?			

Should West bid 3♠? Much of the time it is best to pass and defend. However, when your side has nine trumps, it will usually work out well to compete at the three-level. Playing five-card majors, the partnership will always be in a position to know whether nine trumps are present.

Playing four-card suits, the raise to the two-level is common with just three trumps. Where opener has five trumps, opener cannot be sure whether nine trumps are there. If opener passes, responder, with four trumps cannot be certain whether opener has only four trumps or has elected to pass with five in case responder has only three. This reduces three-level competitive bidding to guesswork.

• Playing four-card suits often lands you in a 4–3 trump fit.

If you raise a possible four-card major with just three trumps, you will end in a 4–3 fit if partner is not strong enough to push further. If you fail to raise with three trumps, you may miss a 5–3 fit when partner rebids no-trumps and you do not have enough strength to push higher.

The mathematics is strongly against playing in a 4–3 trump fit, even at the lower levels. With a 5–3 trump fit, the chances for a good trump break are about 2-in-3, a bad break 1-in-3. Playing in a 4–3 trump fit, the chance for a good break is only about 1-in-3 and for a bad break 2-in-3. In other words, playing in a 4–3 trump suit doubles your chances of hitting a bad break.

The moral: Five-card majors improve your chances of success and relieve tension. Play five-card majors and live longer!

Part 1   Standard Methods

System Summary

Openings

1♣/1♢	At least a 3-card suit.
1♡/1♠	At least a 5-card suit in first or second seat. Strong 4-card suit in the third/fourth seat allowed.
1NT	15–17 HCP.
2NT	21–22 HCP.
3NT	Gambling.
2♠/2♡	Weak two, 6–10 HCP and strong 6-card suit.
2♢	23 HCP, normally a game-force.
2♣	8½–9½ playing tricks, 21–22 points unbalanced or 19–20 plus a 6-card suit or 9 playing tricks if less than 19 HCP.
Pre-empts	Standard.

Responses to 1♡/1♠

2-level raise: 6–9 points, 3+ trumps.
3-level raise: 10–12 points, 4+ trumps.
1NT: 6–9 HCP.
2NT: 11–12 HCP, 4–3–3–3 pattern.
3NT: 13–15 HCP, 4–3–3–3 pattern.

Responses to 1♣/1♢

1♣:2♣: 6–9 points, 5+ clubs, no major.
1♢:2♢: 6–9 points, 4+ diamonds, no major.
1♣:3♣: 10–12 points, 5+ clubs, no major.
1♢:3♢: 10–12 points, 4+ diamonds, no major.
The responses in no-trumps have the same range as over a major suit opening but any no-trump response denies a 4-card major.

Responses to 1NT

2♣ Stayman. Other 2-level responses weak, not encouraging.

Responses to 2NT

3♣ Stayman. Other 3-level responses natural and forcing.

Responses to 2♣ and 2♢

Next suit up artificial negative (0–7 points). Suit responses natural and 8+ points. 2NT = 8+ points, balanced, unlimited.

Chapter 2

The One Heart and One Spade Openings

In first or second seat, opening One Heart or One Spade promises at least a five-card suit. In third seat a powerful four-card suit (K-Q-J-x or better is acceptable) in order to suggest a useful lead to partner.

The expected point count is 12–20 high card points. Above 20 is too strong with a five-card suit and even 20 may be too much if the hand is distributional. Opening these stronger hands is covered in Chapters 5 and 6.

Opening 1♡ or 1♠ with 11 HCP is acceptable if you have two five-card suits or a six-card suit. 11 HCP hands should also be opened if you have three quick tricks (ace-king plus an ace).

A hand with 10 HCP may be opened 1♡ or 1♠ only with a freak shape (6–5 pattern) or with a seven-card suit if the hand is not suitable for a pre-empt. If most of the high-card strength is in the seven-card suit, a pre-empt is the preferred opening. If at least half of your high card values are outside your long suit, prefer a one-opening and keep rebidding your long suit.

WHICH SUIT TO OPEN?

If you hold a five-card or longer suit:

1. Open your longer suit (even if it is a minor).
2. With two five-card suits or two six-card suits, open the higher-ranking suit.

Exercise

For each of the following hands, what action would you take as dealer?

1. ♠ AJ4
    ♡ K9752
    ◇ Q8
    ♣ J97

2. ♠ KQJ76
    ♡ 8
    ◇ A98732
    ♣ 2

3. ♠ A9742
    ♡ KQJ97
    ◇ K3
    ♣ 6

4. ♠ KQ862
    ♡ 4
    ◇ K9
    ♣ KQ862

5. ♠ Q97542
    ♡ 2
    ◇ AKJ762
    ♣ ---

6. ♠ AK3
    ♡ 87432
    ◇ KQJ9
    ♣ 7

7. ♠ 5
    ♡ K986532
    ◇ AQJ
    ♣ 72

8. ♠ 7
    ♡ AKJ9865
    ◇ Q85
    ♣ 72

9. ♠ KQJ1072
    ♡ 7
    ◇ QJ986
    ♣ 4

10. ♠ A97
    ♡ AK542
    ◇ 75
    ♣ 732

11. ♠ KQJ73
    ♡ AKJ732
    ◇ 6
    ♣ 4

12. ♠ K8742
    ♡ J86432
    ◇ A
    ♣ A

RESPONDING TO PARTNER'S 1♡ OR 1♠ OPENING

Order of priorities if your hand fits different choices:

With a weak hand (6–9 points):
1. Support partner's major (1♡:2♡ or 1♠:2♠).
2. Respond 1♠ over a 1♡ opening.
3. Bid 1NT (last choice).

With a strong hand (10 points or more):
1. Jump-raise opener's major (four trumps required).
2. Change suit.
3. Bid 2NT or 3NT (strict requirements).

1♡:2♡ or 1♠:2♠
At least three-card support and 6–9 points.

1♡:3♡ or 1♠:3♠
At least four-card support, 10–12 points and eight losers. With the same values and only three-card support, change suit and raise on the next round.

1♡:4♡ or 1♠:4♠
At least four-card support, up to 9 HCP, a singleton or a void somewhere and seven losers. Any better hand is too strong for this shut-out raise.

   With support for opener and 13 points or more (or seven losers or better), change suit first and jump to game on the next round (13–15 points) or jump-shift first (16 points or more) and support opener on the next round.

Counting Losers
A minimum opening hand will usually have seven losers or fewer. For any three-card or longer suit, count a loser for each ace, king or queen missing in this suit. Count two losers for any doubleton except for A-x or K-x (1-loser) or A-K (no loser). Count one loser for any singleton except ace-singleton (no loser). A void counts as no losers. A trump fit and 14 losers in the combined hands will usually produce ten tricks (opening hand – 7 losers, opposite opening hand – 7 losers).

Exercise

A. Partner has opened One Heart. Your response?

1.	♠ K83	2.	♠ KQ7	3.	♠ 72
	♡ K97		♡ A983		♡ A95
	◇ Q632		◇ J1074		◇ K542
	♣ 752		♣ 62		♣ QJ83

4.	♠ 6	5.	♠ QJ75	6.	♠ KQ983
	♡ K8643		♡ Q62		♡ 764
	◇ A9542		◇ J8		◇ Q6
	♣ 74		♣ 7632		♣ 753

B. Partner has opened One Spade. Your response?

1.	♠ KJ4	2.	♠ KQ7	3.	♠ KQ93
	♡ K9873		♡ K4		♡ 432
	◇ 76		◇ J982		◇ KQ2
	♣ 652		♣ A1073		♣ A76

4.	♠ A8762	5.	♠ AJ8	6.	♠ A82
	♡ KQJ		♡ 7432		♡ A76
	◇ 43		◇ 432		◇ 984
	♣ AQ9		♣ AQ7		♣ Q742

1♡ or 1♠ : 2NT

A 4–3–3–3 pattern and 11–12 HCP with stoppers in the unbid suits. Denies four cards in the other major.

Opener is allowed to pass or raise to 3NT. If opener rebids three-of-the-opened major, this is a sign-off. All other actions below game are forcing. A change of suit suggests slam aspirations, otherwise opener would sign off in 4-Major.

1♡ or 1♠ : 3NT

Same as 2NT but the point count is 13–15. If you lack the stoppers for a response of 2NT or 3NT, change suit first and either support opener's major or rebid no-trumps on the next round.

With a balanced hand and 16 HCP or more, start with a change of suit.

1♡ : 1♠

Shows at least four spades and 6 points or more. Forcing for one round.

Suit Responses at the Two Level

These are forcing for one round. The expectancy is 10 points or more and at least a four-card suit. 9 HCP will do if the minor is a six-card suit. A three-card suit is feasible if you plan to support opener on the next round.

When changing suit:
- Bid your longer suit first.
- With two five-card suits, bid the higher-ranking first.
- With four-card suits, bid the cheapest suit first.

1♠ : 2♡ shows 10 or more points and at least five hearts. Opener should support the hearts at once with three or more trumps. Any other rebid by opener would imply fewer than three hearts.

Jump Shifts

The expectancy is 16 HCP or more and at least a four-card suit.

Exercise

A. Partner has opened One Heart. Your response?

1.	♠ K97 ♡ K43 ♢ KJ6 ♣ J1093	2.	♠ K97 ♡ K43 ♢ 642 ♣ AJ103	3.	♠ K9 ♡ K43 ♢ KJ64 ♣ J1043
4.	♠ AJ5 ♡ Q93 ♢ A104 ♣ K753	5.	♠ AJ5 ♡ Q93 ♢ 742 ♣ AK53	6.	♠ A532 ♡ 93 ♢ 742 ♣ AK53

B. Partner has opened One Spade. Your response?

1.	♠ 76 ♡ J52 ♢ J8 ♣ KQ10732	2.	♠ 7 ♡ A92 ♢ 972 ♣ KQ10732	3.	♠ 6 ♡ K982 ♢ Q854 ♣ Q972
4.	♠ 7 ♡ AQ84 ♢ KQ93 ♣ K1072	5.	♠ 983 ♡ AK43 ♢ 652 ♣ K97	6.	♠ 9 ♡ Q7 ♢ AJ862 ♣ KQ542

OPENER'S REBIDS

AFTER 1♡:2♡ or 1♠:2♠

Bid game with 19 HCP or more or 5 losers or fewer.

With 16–18 HCP try for game. Raise to the three level or bid a new suit as a trial bid where help is needed. A typical trial suit is three or four cards long with one top honour or no top honour.

Under 16 HCP, pass unless your hand is worth six losers. If so, try for game as above. Under 16 points and seven losers: Pass.

AFTER 1♡:3♡ or 1♠:3♠

Pass with a balanced hand of 12–13 points. With 14 points or better, bid game. Bid game also if minimum when you have a singleton or a void. Slam is feasible with 19 HCP or more or a hand of four losers.

AFTER 1♡:4♡ or 1♠:4♠

Pass unless there are slam prospects (four losers and control in at least three suits).

AFTER 1♡ or 1♠:1NT

Pass if 5–3–3–2 and 12–15 points. Raise to 2NT with 16–18 and 3NT with 19+. Bid a new suit with other patterns or rebid your major with a six-card suit.

AFTER 1♡ or 1♠:2NT

Bid 3♡/3♠ with 12–13 balanced. Bid game with 14 points or more, choosing 3NT with a 5–3–3–2 pattern. With 12–13 points and a singleton or a void, also take a shot at game.

AFTER 1♡ or 1♠:3NT

Pass with a 5–3–3–2 pattern unless you have slam prospects. Bid game in your major with an unbalanced hand and no hopes for slam.

AFTER 1♡:1♠

Raise spades with four trumps. Otherwise, rebid no-trumps with a 5–3–3–2 pattern, bid a new suit or rebid hearts with six.

AFTER 1♡ or 1♠:2-minor

Raise partner with four trumps. With a minimum, bid a new suit below your major. Without such a suit, rebid your major. Rebid 2NT with 15–18 (forcing to game) or 3NT with 19-up and 5–3–3–2.

Exercise

A.   WEST   EAST
  1♡   1♠
  ?   What should opener rebid on these hands?

    1.   ♠ A7   2.   ♠ K982   3.   ♠ 82
       ♡ AQ752   ♡ AK8732   ♡ AJ853
       ◇ K98   ◇ AQ   ◇ KJ108
       ♣ K32   ♣ 4   ♣ A2

B.   WEST   EAST
  1♡   3♡
  ?   What should opener rebid on these hands?

    1.   ♠ AJ   2.   ♠ A5   3.   ♠ 9852
       ♡ KQJ53   ♡ K9752   ♡ AK863
       ◇ 985   ◇ AQJ   ◇ AJ9
       ♣ J53   ♣ 532   ♣ 2

C.   WEST   EAST
  1♠   1NT
  ?   What should opener rebid on these hands?

    1.   ♠ KQ982   2.   ♠ AJ762   3.   ♠ KQ853
       ♡ AJ7   ♡ AQ6   ♡ KJ62
       ◇ 98   ◇ KQ   ◇ KJ72
       ♣ K93   ♣ K102   ♣ ---

D.   WEST   EAST
  1♠   2◇
  ?   What should opener rebid on these hands?

    1.   ♠ AJ764   2.   ♠ AJ764   3.   ♠ AJ764
       ♡ K87   ♡ 82   ♡ QJ72
       ◇ 97   ◇ A4   ◇ 9
       ♣ KQ4   ♣ A832   ♣ A72

RESPONDER'S REBIDS

AFTER 1♡:1♠, 1NT REBID BY OPENER
With a minimum hand, pass if balanced or bid a suit at the two level otherwise.

With a strong hand, raise no-trumps if balanced or jump bid a suit to the three level, forcing to game.

AFTER OPENER REBIDS 2-MINOR
After responding 1NT

With a weak hand, pass or give preference to opener's major or bid a new suit (e.g. 1♡:1NT, 2♣:2◇). This new suit rebid denies support for opener's suits and the expectancy is at least a six-card suit.

AFTER 1♡:1♠, 2♣:2◇
Responder with 6–9 points may pass, give preference to opener's major or rebid 2♠ with a six-card suit (or a very strong five-card suit). With 10–12 points, raise one of opener's suits to the three level, jump-rebid 3♠ with a six-card suit or rebid 2NT. With 13 points or more, rebid game or bid the other minor (fourth-suit forcing).

Fourth-Suit Forcing
If responder uses fourth-suit forcing, opener should make a descriptive minimum rebid with a weak opening (responder may pass this) or a jump rebid with a strongish opening (14 HCP or more). The jump by opener creates a force to game. If responder bids again after a minimum reply by opener to the fourth suit, the auction is forcing to game.

AFTER RESPONDER'S TWO-LEVEL NEW SUIT REPLY
Responder has already shown 10 points or more by the two-level response. If opener rebids 2NT or jump bids (e.g., 1♠:2◇, 3♠ or 1♠:2◇, 4◇) a game force has been created. If opener rebids the suit opened (minimum hand) or a suit at the two level below the suit opened (e.g., 1♠:2♣, 2♡ — forcing but may be a minimum opening), responder may support opener's major (invitational), rebid 2NT (invitational), rebid responder's suit (9–11 HCP and a six-card suit) or bid a new suit (forcing) or bid game.

Exercise

A.   WEST   EAST
  1♡   1♠
  2♣   ?   What should East rebid on these hands?

 1. ♠ K872   2. ♠ K872   3. ♠ KQ54
     ♡ J6   ♡ J6   ♡ J6
     ◇ Q75   ◇ Q75   ◇ AQ5
     ♣ J753   ♣ AJ53   ♣ J542

 4. ♠ AJ832   5. ♠ K9742   6. ♠ K9742
     ♡ 8   ♡ Q3   ♡ Q3
     ◇ AQ985   ◇ Q84   ◇ AQ4
     ♣ Q8   ♣ 762   ♣ 762

B.   WEST   EAST
  1♡   2♣
  2◇   ?   What should East rebid on these hands?

 1. ♠ Q32   2. ♠ K2   3. ♠ 82
     ♡ Q94   ♡ 72   ♡ 72
     ◇ 72   ◇ 863   ◇ AQ54
     ♣ AQ842   ♣ KQJ975   ♣ AKJ54

 4. ♠ J82   5. ♠ 942   6. ♠ AQ7
     ♡ 542   ♡ 7   ♡ 82
     ◇ A32   ◇ QJ3   ◇ 764
     ♣ AKQ4   ♣ AKQ876   ♣ AK842

Chapter 3

The No-Trump Openings

1NT: 15–17 HCP and balanced shape. No 5-card major.

2NT: 21–22 HCP and balanced shape. No 5-card major.

Balanced hands of other strengths (no 5-card major):

0–11:   Pass

12–14:   Open 1-minor and rebid 1NT over a 1-level reply, or pass a raise to two of your suit. After 1◇:2♣, the 2NT rebid shows a minimum balanced opening.

18–20:   Open 1-minor and jump rebid no-trumps. The sequence 1-minor followed by a JUMP to 2NT (e.g., 1♣:1♡, 2NT) is played as forcing to game.

23–up: Open 2◇ (showing 23 HCP or more) and rebid no-trumps. After 2◇:2♡ (negative), 2NT shows 23–24 points and 3NT shows 25–27 points.

RESPONDING TO 1NT

2♣:   Stayman asking for a 4-card major. Opener bids 2◇ (no major), 2♡ (4 hearts) or 2♠ (4 spades). With both majors, bid 2♡.

2◇/2♡/2♠:   Intended as sign-offs. 0–7 points, at least a 5-card suit. With a maximum 1NT, support for responder and a doubleton, opener may raise to the three level. Otherwise, opener must pass.

3♣/3◇/3♡/3♠:   Forcing to game with a 5-card or longer suit. 3♣ or 3◇ suggests slam chances.

RESPONDING TO 2NT

3♣:   Stayman, asking for a 4-card major. Opener replies at the three level just as after 1NT:2♣.

3◇/3♡/3♠:   Forcing to game with a 5-card or longer suit. 3◇ suggests slam.

Exercise

A. Partner has opened 1NT. Your response?

1. ♠ AJ72
♡ K9
♢ Q742
♣ 863

2. ♠ AJ762
♡ K9
♢ Q742
♣ 86

3. ♠ AJ8762
♡ K9
♢ Q742
♣ 8

4. ♠ Q83
♡ J10762
♢ 98
♣ 532

5. ♠ A7
♡ 62
♢ KJ2
♣ K97632

6. ♠ KJ7
♡ AJ3
♢ AK62
♣ J86

B. Partner has opened 2NT. Your response?

1. ♠ J876
♡ J5
♢ 8764
♣ 932

2. ♠ KJ7
♡ AQJ
♢ Q983
♣ 752

3. ♠ A7
♡ 52
♢ K86432
♣ 754

4. ♠ J5
♡ QJ64
♢ Q762
♣ 863

5. ♠ 8
♡ J98543.
♢ 953
♣ 72

6. ♠ KQ7
♡ 7
♢ AQ954
♣ 10963

Chapter 4

The One Club and One Diamond Openings

In addition to opening with a five-card or longer minor, the One Club and One Diamond openings cater for the 4–4–3–2, 4–3–3–3 and 4–4–4–1 patterns.

The opening strengths are the same as for opening One Heart or One Spade (see Chapter 2), essentially 12–20 points, but hands weaker in high card points may be opened with freakish shape.

WHICH MINOR TO OPEN?

Open 1NT if the hand fits the requirements. If not, and you hold a five-card or longer suit:

1. Open your longest suit.

2. With two five-card suits or two six-card suits, open the higher-ranking suit.

With no five-card or longer suit (4–4–3–2, 4–3–3–3 or 4–4–4–1 patterns):

3. Open your longer minor suit.

4. With equal length in the minors:

    ● Open 1◇ with 4–4 in the minors.

    ● Open 1♣ with 3–3 in the minors.

The upshot of these rules is that a minor suit opening guarantees three or more cards in the minor. The One Diamond opening for all practical purposes shows a four-card suit and may be supported with four trumps. (It is true that with 4 spades, 4 hearts, 3 diamonds and 2 clubs, you may be opening One Diamond, but this odd case should not deter you from catering for the 99% of cases where the diamond opening will be based on at least a four-card suit.) The One Club opening is frequently a three-card suit and you should support only with five or more trumps.

Exercise

What action would you take as dealer on each of these hands?

1. ♠ 8
   ♡ AQ73
   ♢ KQ54
   ♣ KQ32

2. ♠ AJ76
   ♡ A983
   ♢ KJ65
   ♣ 4

3. ♠ AJ87
   ♡ 5
   ♢ K984
   ♣ AQ32

4. ♠ AJ87
   ♡ KQ8
   ♢ 862
   ♣ K73

5. ♠ AJ87
   ♡ K73
   ♢ KQ8
   ♣ 862

6. ♠ AJ8
   ♡ J74
   ♢ K963
   ♣ KJ4

7. ♠ A872
   ♡ K3
   ♢ QJ84
   ♣ AJ4

8. ♠ A53
   ♡ K3
   ♢ QJ84
   ♣ A743

9. ♠ Q8
   ♡ KJ87
   ♢ QJ84
   ♣ A73

10. ♠ AK4
    ♡ A7
    ♢ 9752
    ♣ QJ43

11. ♠ 8
    ♡ AJ2
    ♢ AJ43
    ♣ QJ762

12. ♠ 8
    ♡ K9
    ♢ K9854
    ♣ AQ873

RESPONDING TO 1♣ OR 1◇ WITH A WEAK HAND (6–9 POINTS)

In order of preference:
1. Bid a new suit at the one level.
2. Support opener's minor.
3. Bid 1NT (last choice).

When bidding a new suit and you have a choice of suits:

- Bid your longest suit first.
- With two five-card suits or two six-card suits, bid the higher-ranking suit first.
- With two or three four-card suits, bid the cheapest suit.

Four-card suits are bid 'up-the-line', five-card suits are bid 'down-the-line'.

The more common errors in responding with a weak hand can be eliminated by following these guidelines:

- Bid a major rather than support a minor.
- Bid a major rather than respond in no-trumps.

Some players have a misguided approach after partner opens One Club and they have a diamond suit as well as a major suit. If the diamonds are longer, respond 1◇. If the suits are both four-card suits, respond 1◇, up-the-line.

This is particularly useful when you have a weak hand. If there is a major suit fit, it allows the stronger hand to bid the major first. It is also possible that a diamond fit exists. If opener has a minimum hand with five clubs and four diamonds, the best contract may be in diamonds. However, if responder fails to show the diamond suit, the diamond fit may go begging.

Exercise

A. Partner has opened One Club. What is your response?

1. ♠ K986 ♡ 5432 ♢ A6 ♣ 652	2. ♠ J984 ♡ A72 ♢ QJ3 ♣ 984	3. ♠ K987 ♡ 76 ♢ 95 ♣ K8753
4. ♠ AJ65 ♡ 64 ♢ Q8532 ♣ 42	5. ♠ 83 ♡ AQ75 ♢ Q542 ♣ 874	6. ♠ 97 ♡ Q6432 ♢ AJ862 ♣ 8

B. Partner has opened One Diamond. What is your response?

1. ♠ AJ98 ♡ Q952 ♢ J764 ♣ 9	2. ♠ 76 ♡ KQ87 ♢ Q8762 ♣ 83	3. ♠ K872 ♡ J4 ♢ 63 ♣ K8742
4. ♠ 76 ♡ 84 ♢ Q7653 ♣ KQ74	5. ♠ 9762 ♡ A8 ♢ QJ3 ♣ 8743	6. ♠ 98 ♡ K65 ♢ Q742 ♣ J872

RESPONDING TO 1♣ OR 1◇ WITH A STRONG HAND (10 POINTS OR MORE)

The basic choices are:

1. Bid a new suit.
2. Bid 2NT or 3NT if the strict requirements are met.
3. Jump raise opener's minor.

When bidding a new suit and you have a choice of suits:

- Bid your longest suit first.
- With two five-card suits or two six-card suits, bid the higher-ranking suit first.
- With two or three four-card suits, bid the cheapest suit.

There are no suit quality requirements. Any four-card or longer suit is biddable.

The 2NT response
This requires 11–12 points, balanced shape, no four-card major and stoppers in each of the unbid suits. If any of these requirements is not present, bid a new suit.

The 3NT response
The requirements are the same as for the 2NT response except that the point count is 13–15.

The jump-raise
This shows 10–12 points, support for opener's minor (four trumps for diamonds, five for clubs) and no four-card major. If the hand fits both the 2NT response and the jump-raise, choose 2NT rather than support the minor.

Hands with support and 13–15 points will often change suit first, continue with fourth-suit-forcing to show the strength and then show the support for opener's minor.

The jump-shift
A jump-shift to a major shows at least a five-card suit and 16 points or more.

Exercise

A. Partner has opened One Club. What is your response?

1. ♠ AJ6   2. ♠ AJ62   3. ♠ AJ6
    ♡ K97   ♡ K97   ♡ 87
    ◇ K86   ◇ K86   ◇ K86
    ♣ 9752   ♣ 975   ♣ K9752

4. ♠ KQ7   5. ♠ 87   6. ♠ KQ7
    ♡ AJ8   ♡ AJ8   ♡ 73
    ◇ K762   ◇ K762   ◇ AJ6
    ♣ 432   ♣ KQJ2   ♣ KJ873

B. Partner has opened One Diamond. What is your response?

1. ♠ KQJ7   2. ♠ AKJ876   3. ♠ AJ874
    ♡ AQ83   ♡ KQJ   ♡ KJ
    ◇ AJ52   ◇ K52   ◇ A8732
    ♣ 4   ♣ 8   ♣ 6

4. ♠ 62   5. ♠ KQ5   6. ♠ AJ632
    ♡ AQJ   ♡ 94   ♡ 4
    ◇ K9762   ◇ QJ73   ◇ 5
    ♣ K83   ♣ K942   ♣ AQ8742

OPENER'S REBID

AFTER 1♣:1◇:
In order of preference:
1. Bid a major.
2. Raise diamonds with four-card support (2◇ 13–15 points, 3◇ 16–18 points).
3. Rebid no-trumps with a balanced hand (1NT 12–14 points, 2NT 18–20 points). The jump to 2NT is forcing to game.
4. Repeat your first suit (2♣ 12–15 points, 3♣ 16–18).

AFTER A MAJOR SUIT RESPONSE:
In order of preference:
1. Support partner's major.
2. Change suit.
3. Rebid in no-trumps.
4. Repeat your first suit.

The Barrier Principle
The only restriction for opener's rebid is that with a minimum opening, opener must not change suit beyond two-of-the-suit-opened. Thus, if you open 1♣, your barrier is 2♣. Change of suit up to 2♣ does not promise extra values (e.g., 1♣:1♡, 1♠), but a new suit beyond 2♣ (e.g., 1♣:1♡, 2◇) implies 16 points or more. A change of suit at the two-level also implies at least five cards in the suit opened. For example, 1◇:1♠, 2♡ indicates opener has four hearts and at least five diamonds.

The Skip-Over Principle
If opener's rebid bypasses a suit, opener denies holding that suit. For example, with 1♣:1◇, 1♡ opener has not denied holding four spades, but with 1♣:1◇, 1♠ opener has denied four hearts as 1♡ was bypassed. Similarly, 1♣:1◇, 1NT denies four hearts and denies four spades (1♡ and 1♠ were both skipped). Likewise, 1◇:1♡, 2◇ denies four spades and denies four clubs.

Exercise

A. WEST   EAST
   1♣   1♢
   ?   What should West rebid on these hands?

1.	2.	3.
♠ KJ74	♠ Q872	♠ QJ7
♡ K862	♡ KQ3	♡ K9
♢ 4	♢ 62	♢ 872
♣ AJ93	♣ AQ62	♣ AK642

4.	5.	6.
♠ AJ7	♠ AJ7	♠ A76
♡ 7	♡ 7	♡ KQ3
♢ K983	♢ K98	♢ KJ2
♣ AKJ93	♣ AKJ974	♣ AQ92

B. WEST   EAST
   1♢   1♠
   ?   What should West rebid on these hands?

1.	2.	3.
♠ A7	♠ 962	♠ 9
♡ KQ3	♡ AKJ4	♡ AJ54
♢ K9742	♢ AJ873	♢ AQJ93
♣ 963	♣ A	♣ 653

4.	5.	6.
♠ 9	♠ 9	♠ KJ74
♡ K63	♡ K6	♡ 7
♢ AQ742	♢ AQ742	♢ AK972
♣ A872	♣ AKQ93	♣ AQ3

RESPONDER'S REBIDS

Responder has 6–9 points

If opener has not made a jump rebid, keep to the one-level or two-level with such a weak hand. You may rebid 1NT or support opener's suit at the two-level or rebid your own suit at the two-level. All of these are weak actions. You may pass a 1NT rebid or a new suit at the two-level, lower-ranking than opener's first suit (e.g., 1♢:1♠, 2♣). You should bid again after a change of suit at the one-level (e.g., 1♢:1♡, 1♠).

If opener has bid beyond the barrier (e.g., 1♣:1♠, 2♡), opener has shown 16 points or more and you must bid again. With a poor hand you may rebid 2NT. 3-of-opener's-suit (either one) or rebid your suit at the two-level.

If opener has not bid beyond the barrier and you have a poor hand, you should not rebid 2NT (e.g., 1♢:1♠, 2♣:2NT indicates 10–12 points with responder) nor raise opener to the three-level (again this shows 10–12 points).

If opener has made a jump rebid in opener's suit (1♣:1♡, 3♣) or in responder's suit (1♣:1♡, 3♡), you should pass with 6–7 points, but keep bidding with 8 points or more.

Responder has 10–12 points

This is enough to invite a game over a minimum rebid by opener. After a 1NT rebid, raise to 2NT with 11–12 points and a balanced hand (pass with a balanced hand and just 10 points as opener's maximum is 14). After a minimum suit rebid, you may rebid 2NT or raise opener to the three-level (1♢:1♡, 1♠:3♠) or jump to the three-level with your own six-card suit (1♢:1♡, 2♣:3♡).

If opener has shown a strong hand (by a jump rebid or by bidding beyond the barrier), you must insist on game with 10 points or better. Even with 9 points, it would be timid to settle for less than game. Bid game if it is clear which game is best. If not, change suit or use fourth-suit-forcing to keep the auction going.

Responder has 13–15 points

Now you have enough points for game even opposite a minimum rebid by opener. Jump to game if the correct game is clear. Change suit to force opener to bid again (after a 1NT rebid by opener, you need to jump to force opener to keep bidding) or make use of fourth-suit-forcing.

Partnership Bidding Practice

How should the following hands be bid? West is the dealer on all the hands.

WEST		EAST		WEST		EAST	
1.	♠ AJ72	1.	♠ 9	7.	♠ 9	7.	♠ KJ742
	♡ 82		♡ A9543		♡ AKJ3		♡ 92
	◇ Q54		◇ 832		◇ AKQ54		◇ J87
	♣ AQ83		♣ K762		♣ 973		♣ J62
2.	♠ QJ53	2.	♠ K842	8.	♠ 87	8.	♠ KQ62
	♡ 742		♡ AKJ3		♡ 43		♡ AJ75
	◇ Q8		◇ 762		◇ AKQ3		◇ 762
	♣ AKJ5		♣ 94		♣ AKJ73		♣ 94
3.	♠ 87	3.	♠ KJ65	9.	♠ K72	9.	♠ 863
	♡ A3		♡ Q976		♡ 4		♡ AKQ3
	◇ QJ4		◇ K7		◇ AJ762		◇ 543
	♣ AKQ872		♣ 543		♣ A1054		♣ KQ2
4.	♠ 98	4.	♠ KQ6	10.	♠ AQJ5	10.	♠ 43
	♡ A3		♡ K742		♡ K42		♡ A9765
	◇ KQ954		◇ 832		◇ Q		◇ K87
	♣ AQ73		♣ K62		♣ A7432		♣ KQJ
5.	♠ AJ75	5.	♠ K3	11.	♠ AQJ5	11.	♠ 43
	♡ J8		♡ KQ10962		♡ 8		♡ AJ765
	◇ AK873		◇ Q6		◇ 973		◇ J84
	♣ 92		♣ J63		♣ AJ432		♣ KQ6
6.	♠ KQ95	6.	♠ 742	12.	♠ AQJ5	12.	♠ 64
	♡ K8		♡ J754		♡ 84		♡ AJ765
	◇ 975		◇ K83		◇ QJ2		◇ 843
	♣ AJ86		♣ Q42		♣ K976		♣ AQ3

Chapter 5

The Two Club Opening

The function of the 2♣ opening is to cater for hands just below game-forcing strength. Hands with 23 HCP or more are opened 2◇, but hands just below that strength are suitable for 2♣. Balanced hands of 21–22 points are opened 2NT but unbalanced hands of that strength would be opened 2♣. If you open with a one-bid, partner may pass with 4–5 points, yet that would be enough for game opposite 21–22 points or the equivalent in playing strength.

Follow this guide and you will have a sound 2♣ opening:

Open 2♣ with:

> 21–22 HCP and at least a 5-card suit
> 19–20 HCP and at least a 6-card suit
> 17–18 HCP and at least a 7-card suit

You may open 2♣ below the above strength with a one-suited hand, provided your hand is worth about nine playing tricks, such as:
♠ AKQ8732 ♡ 62 ◇ AK ♣ 95

You may fudge on the above ranges by 1 HCP but no more than that. With lesser values, choose a one-opening.

You should not open 2♣ with a balanced hand of 18–20 HCP (open one in a suit and jump in no-trumps next round) or a balanced hand of 21–22 points (open 2NT, including 5–3–3–2 hands with a five-card minor). Do not open 2♣ with a two-suiter or three-suiter below 21 HCP. With two- or three-suiters around the 18–20 HCP range, open with a one-bid and jump-shift on the next round.

RESPONDING TO 2♣

2◇ = Artificial negative, 0–6 points. With 7 points made up of an ace and a king or an A-Q-J suit, give a positive response. With other 7-point holdings, give the 2◇ negative response.

All other bids are natural and show 8 points or more (or an

excellent 7). A positive response is forcing to game. Responder will take slam action with sufficient values.

After a negative 2◇, opener's suit rebid indicates at least a five-card suit. Responder is allowed to pass but should bid again with hands of 5–7 points or about one trick or better.

Partnership Bidding

How should the following hands be bid? West is the dealer on all the hands.

WEST		EAST		WEST		EAST	
1.	♠ J3	1.	♠ KQ10854	7.	♠ 954	7.	♠ A3
	♡ 43		♡ QJ6		♡ J52		♡ 763
	◇ AKQ		◇ 743		◇ 843		◇ AKQJ95
	♣ AKQ872		♣ 5		♣ K542		♣ A7
2.	♠ 64	2.	♠ AKQ8752	8.	♠ 832	8.	♠ 64
	♡ 94		♡ 53		♡ 87		♡ AKQJ653
	◇ J732		◇ A6		◇ J653		◇ AQ2
	♣ J6432		♣ A8		♣ 9752		♣ A
3.	♠ 532	3.	♠ AK	9.	♠ KJ	9.	♠ Q3
	♡ 87		♡ AKQ9532		♡ AJ109765		♡ K842
	◇ A754		◇ 86		◇ AKQ		◇ 84
	♣ 8532		♣ 94		♣ 7		♣ AKQ64
4.	♠ A42	4.	♠ 7	10.	♠ AQJ1087	10.	♠ 542
	♡ AKQJ872		♡ 653		♡ AKQ		♡ 6
	◇ A7		◇ 96532		◇ A74		◇ J852
	♣ 7		♣ 8532		♣ 8		♣ AKQJ4
5.	♠ A42	5.	♠ 653	11.	♠ J9875	11.	♠ 3
	♡ AKQJ872		♡ 6		♡ 54		♡ AJ2
	◇ A7		◇ 96532		◇ 62		◇ KQJ9843
	♣ 7		♣ 8532		♣ 9873		♣ AK
6.	♠ A8	6.	♠ 7632	12.	♠ 4	12.	♠ 86532
	♡ 743		♡ J852		♡ A6		♡ K75
	◇ A		◇ 7643		◇ AK		◇ 743
	♣ AKQJ982		♣ 4		♣ KQJ87542		♣ 63

Chapter 6

The Two Diamond Opening

Benjamin Twos, named after Albert Benjamin of Glasgow, feature a 2◇ opening to cover powerhouse hands. All hands with 23 HCP or more are opened 2◇. Except for one sequence, the 2◇ opening leads to game. If partner has nothing and game fails, so be it. Better to bid game and fail occasionally than to stop below game when game can be made.

You may also open 2◇ below 23 HCP if your hand has ten playing tricks (three losers) and a long major, or better than ten playing tricks when your long suit is a minor.

RESPONDING TO 2◇

2♡ = Artificial negative, 0–6 points or a poor 7.

All others = 8 points or more (or 7 points consisting of an ace and a king or an A-Q-J suit). The function of the positive response is to indicate values which will make slam likely. The negative response indicates less than 1½ quick tricks (*see* p.44) and thus less than slam potential if opener has only ten tricks (three losers).

A suit response is played as a five-card suit and 2NT shows a balanced positive with no major. A response of 3♡ is necessary to show a positive response with five or more hearts.

2◇:2♡, 2NT = 23–24 points balanced. Responder may pass this rebid. If responder does bid, the auctions are the same as though opener had started with 2NT (3♣ Stayman, other suits at the three-level are five-card suits and forcing).

After 2◇:2♡, all rebids other than 2NT commit the partnership to game. The first genuine suit bid by opener over 2♡ is taken as a five-card suit. Responder's first genuine suit after the initial 2♡ negative is also taken as a five-card suit. After opener's rebid, responder would support opener if possible, otherwise bid a five-card or longer suit or rebid no-trumps.

After 2◇:2NT (balanced positive), 3♣ is Stayman and other

suits are natural, at least five cards long. Bidding is natural and should lead to slam if a trump fit is found or either partner has more than the minimum requirements.

Partnership Bidding

How should the following hands be bid? West is the dealer each time.

WEST	EAST	WEST	EAST
1. ♠ 8 ♡ 7653 ♢ 8432 ♣ 7652	1. ♠ AKQ94 ♡ AKQ2 ♢ AK ♣ 98	7. ♠ AKQ732 ♡ A86 ♢ AK ♣ A8	7. ♠ — ♡ 975432 ♢ 9864 ♣ J53
2. ♠ AKQ8764 ♡ KQJ ♢ AK ♣ Q	2. ♠ 532 ♡ A7 ♢ 62 ♣ A87543	8. ♠ AKJ2 ♡ 3 ♢ 42 ♣ 1098742	8. ♠ 8 ♡ AKQJ2 ♢ AQJ ♣ KQJ3
3. ♠ J964 ♡ K8 ♢ 98 ♣ 76532	3. ♠ AK10752 ♡ QJ2 ♢ AKQ ♣ A	9. ♠ AKJ ♡ A943 ♢ AK85 ♣ A2	9. ♠ 863 ♡ K5 ♢ Q3 ♣ KQJ1074
4. ♠ QJ64 ♡ 8743 ♢ 98 ♣ J43	4. ♠ AK10752 ♡ QJ2 ♢ AKQ ♣ A	10. ♠ AKQ872 ♡ AKQ93 ♢ 2 ♣ A	10. ♠ 4 ♡ J7654 ♢ A653 ♣ 974
5. ♠ KQJ ♡ AKJ93 ♢ AK6 ♣ A10	5. ♠ A73 ♡ 42 ♢ Q94 ♣ K9632	11. ♠ QJ62 ♡ 87 ♢ 8732 ♣ 973	11. ♠ K984 ♡ AK94 ♢ AKQ ♣ A5
6. ♠ QJ2 ♡ 975 ♢ 8642 ♣ 984	6. ♠ AK3 ♡ 862 ♢ AKQ9 ♣ AK7	12. ♠ J8762 ♡ Q952 ♢ 64 ♣ 43	12. ♠ A5 ♡ AK63 ♢ KQJ ♣ AK52

Chapter 7

Opening Two Hearts or Two Spades

Weak twos are popular because of their frequency compared with strong twos. The best way to consider a weak two is as a pre-empt with just a six-card suit. In first or second seat, the requirements are:
- 6–10 HCP.
- Strong six-card suit (at least 3 points in the suit).
- No void and not two singletons.

The possible shapes then are 6–3–2–2, 6–3–3–1 and 6–4–2–1 provided that the four-card suit is a minor. Do not pre-empt with a side four-card major. With 11 HCP or more, open with a one-bid.

In third seat, these requirements are relaxed. A powerful five-card suit is acceptable, the point count may vary by a point or so and the presence of a void does not eliminate the bid. In fourth seat, the shape requirements are the same but the point count is 8–12, a practical range.

RESPONDING TO 2♡ or 2♠

- Raising opener's suit is weak, pre-emptive. Opener should pass.
- Change of suit is forcing and implies no fit for opener's major. The minimum strength for a change of suit with a misfit is 16 HCP and a good five-card or longer suit.
- 2NT (the Ogust Convention) is used as an enquiry bid for hands worth an invitation to game or worth slam investigation.

A weak two opener has about six tricks if maximum, five tricks if minimum (or seven losers maximum, eight losers minimum). With support for opener but no ruffing values, 2NT is suitable with better than three winners. With five winners, just bid game and with more than five winners, slam is possible and again 2NT is a useful enquiry. With support and some ruffing potential, pass with eight losers, use 2NT with seven losers, bid game with six losers and use 2NT for slam exploration with five losers or better.

Opener's replies to 2NT are:

3♣ = Minimum, suit headed by A, K or Q
3◇ = Minimum, suit headed by AK, AQ or KQ
3♡ = Maximum, suit headed by A, K or Q
3♠ = Maximum, suit headed by AK, AQ or KQ
3NT = Maximum, suit headed by A-K-Q
The memory guide based on top honours held is 1–2, 1–2–3.

Partnership Bidding

How should the following hands be bid? West is the dealer each time.

WEST	EAST	WEST	EAST
1. ♠ 65	1. ♠ 874	7. ♠ 84	7. ♠ AQ97
♡ KQ9643	♡ A85	♡ AQJ543	♡ 6
◇ K83	◇ AQ76	◇ 98	◇ KQ765
♣ 42	♣ KQ9	♣ J103	♣ K42
2. ♠ AK8632	2. ♠ Q975	8. ♠ 76	8. ♠ AKQ4
♡ 432	♡ 7	♡ AQ9865	♡ J32
◇ 8	◇ AK93	◇ K3	◇ A942
♣ 643	♣ K852	♣ 842	♣ 96
3. ♠ AJ9643	3. ♠ K8752	9. ♠ 95	9. ♠ A832
♡ 432	♡ 75	♡ AK9863	♡ Q74
◇ 72	◇ 8	◇ 862	◇ A93
♣ K10	♣ Q9743	♣ 73	♣ A54
4. ♠ AQ9642	4. ♠ K7	10. ♠ AKQ864	10. ♠ 9752
♡ J96	♡ AK43	♡ 95	♡ A32
◇ 84	◇ QJ97	◇ 863	◇ A74
♣ 53	♣ KQ10	♣ 74	♣ KQJ
5. ♠ 863	5. ♠ AK54	11. ♠ KQ9642	11. ♠ A103
♡ AJ9753	♡ 62	♡ A3	♡ Q5
◇ 7	◇ AJ32	◇ 97	◇ AKQJ10
♣ Q98	♣ KJ2	♣ 832	♣ A107
6. ♠ 872	6. ♠ 6	12. ♠ AQ9742	12. ♠ J105
♡ KQJ954	♡ A72	♡ 7	♡ 8632
◇ J3	◇ AK42	◇ Q42	◇ K9
♣ 82	♣ AKQ74	♣ 862	♣ A943

Chapter 8

Pre-emptive Openings

The suit opening bids of 3♣ and higher follow the traditional approach based on the Rule of Two and Three.

When vulnerable, open two more than your playing tricks.

When not vulnerable, open three more than your playing tricks.

Playing tricks = 13 minus your losers.

The pre-empts start with 3♣ and go as high as 5◇. Do not pre-empt above game. Counting weak twos, there are three pre-empts in each suit: 2♠/3♠/4♠, 2♡/3♡/4♡, 3◇/4◇/5◇ and 3♣/4♣/5♣. The level you choose depends on your playing tricks and the vulnerability.

A pre-emptive opening should be weak (up to a maximum of 10 HCP) and based on a strong seven-card or longer suit. Even 10 HCP may be too much for a pre-empt. With at least half your HCP outside your long suit, choose a one-opening with 10 HCP and a seven-card or longer suit.

Do not pre-empt in first or second seat with a four-card major on the side.

In third or fourth seat or after an opponent has opened, you may jump to 4♡ or 4♠ with eight playing tricks and up to 15 HCP. The chances for a slam are remote after partner has passed or an opponent has opened the bidding.

RESPONDING TO A PRE-EMPT

Add your quick tricks to those shown by partner. If not enough for game, pass. If enough for game but not slam, bid game. If enough for a slam, bid slam, checking for aces if necessary.

Responder's change of suit below game is forcing.

Quick Tricks outside partner's suit:

    A-K = 2, A-Q = 1½, A = 1, K-Q = 1, K = ½

Tricks for partner:

    In the trump suit: A = 1, K = 1, Q = 1

    Trump support and a singleton: + 1

    Trump support and a void   : + 2

After 3♣ or 3◇, bid 3NT with a balanced hand, stoppers in the unbid suits and about 16 HCP or better if there are no prospects for slam.

Exercise

A. How many playing tricks are each of these suits worth?

1. KQJ7643
2. A9765432
3. AK87653

4. AKQ87642
5. K986542
6. 98765432

7. AQJ8762
8. AQJ87632
9. QJ98753

B. You are the dealer. What action do you take with each of these hands if you are (i) not vulnerable? (ii) vulnerable?

1. ♠ QJ87642
   ♡ 9
   ◇ A73
   ♣ 62

2. ♠ 7
   ♡ AKQ9743
   ◇ 73
   ♣ 875

3. ♠ 8
   ♡ AK97542
   ◇ 73
   ♣ AJ5

4. ♠ KQJ97643
   ♡ —
   ◇ QJ7
   ♣ 53

5. ♠ KQ97542
   ♡ A983
   ◇ 4
   ♣ 6

6. ♠ KQJ1062
   ♡ 4
   ◇ QJ1087
   ♣ 5

C. Partner has opened Three Clubs, not vulnerable. Second player passes. What action do you take?

1. ♠ KQ93
   ♡ AJ87
   ◇ AQ
   ♣ 732

2. ♠ AK3
   ♡ AK8762
   ◇ 53
   ♣ Q2

3. ♠ 98732
   ♡ —
   ◇ AJ97
   ♣ Q872

THE 3NT OPENING

Most systems do not use the 3NT opening in a natural sense. With such a strong hand, it works better to open with a game-force of 2♣ or 2♢ and explore the correct game at a lower level.

The Gambling 3NT is popular. This is a pre-emptive opening based on a solid seven-card or longer minor (AKQxxxx or better) with no outside king or ace. The theory is that the minor suit will provide seven tricks and partner is expected to provide both the stoppers in the outside suits and two or more winners.

Opener should not hold any ace, king or Q-J-x or better in any suit outside the long suit, as this would provide a stopper of which partner would not be aware. Responder then may not be able to judge whether to leave 3NT in or whether to run to opener's minor at the four- or five-level. With as much as a supported queen outside the long suit, choose an opening bid of one.

RESPONDING TO THE GAMBLING 3NT

Responder should pass 3NT with stoppers in the outside suits and a reasonable expectation of scoring two tricks. Responder will normally be able to tell which suit opener holds. If not, responder must be very weak in both minors and should not leave opener in 3NT. It would also be unwise in the extreme to leave 3NT in if you are void in one of the minors. There is no entry to partner's long suit if the contract is no-trumps.

If you judge that 3NT is not the best spot and there is no chance for game, bid partner's suit at the four-level (4♣ or 4♢). If you cannot tell which minor opener holds, bid 4♣. Opener will pass with clubs and bid 4♢ with diamonds.

A bid of 4♡ or 4♠ by responder is to play. If you feel game in opener's minor is a better chance than 3NT, bid opener's suit at the five-level. Again, if you are not sure of the suit, bid 5♣. Opener will pass with clubs and correct to 5♢ with diamonds. You may also wish to jump to the five-level to increase the pre-empt. You may have sufficient values to jump to slam either in opener's minor or no-trumps.

Partnership Bidding

How should the following hands be bid? West is the dealer each time. Neither side is vulnerable.

	WEST		EAST		WEST		EAST
1.	♠ QJ98642 ♡ A ◇ 983 ♣ 62	1.	♠ — ♡ KJ862 ◇ KQ7 ♣ K8543	7.	♠ QJ82 ♡ AJ93 ◇ 43 ♣ 985	7.	♠ 65 ♡ 42 ◇ AKQ9752 ♣ 73
2.	♠ KQJ8763 ♡ — ◇ 863 ♣ 752	2.	♠ A54 ♡ AKQJ2 ◇ A54 ♣ A9	8.	♠ — ♡ 86 ◇ AKQJ862 ♣ 9853	8.	♠ KQJ8 ♡ QJ9 ◇ 54 ♣ KJ64
3.	♠ 9 ♡ AJ107432 ◇ QJ6 ♣ 52	3.	♠ A87642 ♡ 6 ◇ AK42 ♣ A9	9.	♠ 9 ♡ 874 ◇ 93 ♣ AKQ7643	9.	♠ KJ763 ♡ — ◇ J742 ♣ 9852
4.	♠ 62 ♡ — ◇ AK9865432 ♣ J3	4.	♠ 7543 ♡ A98 ◇ J ♣ AQ752	10.	♠ 873 ♡ 7 ◇ 64 ♣ AKQJ542	10.	♠ 62 ♡ AKJ6 ◇ AK95 ♣ 983
5.	♠ J7 ♡ 5 ◇ 983 ♣ AK86532	5.	♠ K982 ♡ AQ7 ◇ AK4 ♣ 974	11.	♠ 76 ♡ 72 ◇ AKQ8652 ♣ 93	11.	♠ AQ94 ♡ K93 ◇ J4 ♣ AKQ10
6.	♠ AQJ8762 ♡ 76 ◇ 43 ♣ 86	6.	♠ 94 ♡ KQ8 ◇ AK65 ♣ A942	12.	♠ 64 ♡ 32 ◇ 87 ♣ AKQ9742	12.	♠ AK5 ♡ AKQ64 ◇ A62 ♣ 103

Part 2   Duplicate Methods

System Summary

Openings
1♣/1◇	At least a 3-card suit
1♡/1♠	At least a 5-card suit in first or second seat. Strong 4-card suit allowed in 3rd/4th seat
1NT	15–17
2NT	21–22
3NT	Specific ace ask
2♡/2♠	Strong two, 8½–9½ playing tricks
2◇	Multi: Weak two in a major OR Acol two in a minor OR 23–24 balanced
2♣	Game-force, 23 HCP or more unbalanced or 25 HCP or more balanced
Pre-empts	Standard

Responses to 1♡/1♠
2-level raise: 6–9 points, 3+ trumps, 9 losers
3-level raise: 6–9 HCP, 4+ trumps, 8 losers
2NT: Strong raise, 10 HCP or more, 4+ trumps
1NT: 6–9 points
3NT: 15–17 points, 4–3–3–3 pattern
Double jumps as splinters

Responses to 1♣/1◇
Same as above responses to 1♡/1♠, but raising opener's minor or a response in no-trumps denies a 4-card major
Responder's 2♣ game try rebid after opener's 1-level rebid

Responses to 1NT and 2NT: Stayman and transfers

Slam bidding: Roman Key Card Blackwood

Competitive methods
Negative doubles. Responsive doubles. Unusual 2NT.
Michaels Cue Bid. Weak jump overcalls

Chapter 9

The One Heart and One Spade Openings

THE RAISE STRUCTURE

Direct raises are based on support and playing strength

1♡:2♡ or 1♠:2♠ shows 3+ support, 6–9 points and 9 losers.
1♡:3♡ or 1♠:3♠ shows 4+ support, 6–9 points and 8 losers.
The hand will normally contain a singleton or two doubletons.
1♡:4♡ or 1♠:4♠ shows 4+ support, 6–9 points an unbalanced hand and 7 losers.

The jumps to the 3-level or 4-level may have a lower high card content if the playing strength is correct but should not contain 10 HCP or more. The stronger raises are shown via 2NT.

1♡:2NT or 1♠:2NT

All strong raises are shown by responding 2NT. If opener is weak, 12–13 points and 7 losers or worse, opener bids 3-Major which responder will pass with a bare minimum. Responder will bid on with extra values. With slam potential, responder may bid a new suit (cue bid) or bid 3NT (Blackwood).

If opener has game values but no slam prospects, opener will bid 4-Major. Responder may bid on via a new suit (cue bid) or 4NT (Blackwood). If opener has slam prospects immediately on hearing the 2NT response, opener may bid a new suit beyond 3-Major (e.g., 1♡:2NT, 3♠ or 1♠:2NT, 4♢) as a cue bid or 3NT as Blackwood.

If opener is not sure of game or needs help in a particular suit for game or for slam, opener may bid a new suit cheaper than 3-Major (e.g., 1♡:2NT, 3♣ or 1♠:2NT, 3♡). If minimum with no help in the trial suit, responder bids 3-Major. With game values, responder bids 4-Major and with slam potential, responder may cue bid above 3-Major or Blackwood with 3NT.

Splinters

Double jumps are splinters, game-forcing raises with a singleton or a void in the suit bid (e.g., 1♥:3♠/4♣/4♦ or 1♠:4♣/4♦/4♥). Responder will have 10 HCP or more and 7 losers or fewer. Opener is asked to judge slam prospects.

Exercise

A.   Partner has opened One Heart. What is your response?

1.	♠ A7	2.	♠ 87	3.	♠ 7
	♥ K872		♥ K72		♥ AJ93
	♦ 98542		♦ AQ872		♦ A876
	♣ 63		♣ Q75		♣ A952

4.	♠ KQ7	5.	♠ A7	6.	♠ 8
	♥ AJ94		♥ KQ932		♥ Q932
	♦ 8732		♦ Q53		♦ KJ72
	♣ 93		♣ AK4		♣ 7642

B.   You opened One Spade and partner responded 2NT. What action do you take with these hands?

1.	♠ AJ752	2.	♠ AQ642	3.	♠ KQJ65
	♥ KQJ		♥ AK3		♥ 7
	♦ K9		♦ AQ		♦ KQ9
	♣ J102		♣ 974		♣ KQJ3

4.	♠ KJ762	5.	♠ Q8642	6.	♠ AQJ62
	♥ A7		♥ KQ		♥ A7
	♦ KJ5		♦ Q763		♦ 7
	♣ 863		♣ A2		♣ AJ754

TREATMENT OF BALANCED HANDS

The 1NT response
This is the standard 6–9 range. Over 1♡, 1NT denies four spades. Bidding proceeds along traditional lines.

10–12 points balanced
Change suit and rebid 2NT, inviting game. A particularly strong 12 count, with tens and nines as fillers, may rebid 3NT.

13–14 points balanced
Change suit and rebid 3NT. If the 3NT rebid is a problem, change suit again or use fourth-suit-forcing.

15–17 points balanced
Jump to 3NT with a 4–3–3–3 pattern (the four-card suit must be a minor) and let opener judge slam prospects. With other patterns, change suit first and continue with 3NT (with no slam potential) or fourth-suit-forcing if the best contract is still not certain.

18 or more balanced
Change suit and if no fit comes to light after opener's rebid, change suit again or use fourth-suit-forcing. With just 18–19 points balanced, settle for game if opener shows a minimum after fourth-suit-forcing, but proceed to slam if opener shows better than minimum points. With 20 HCP or more opposite an opening hand you should be prepared to bid at least a small slam. Choose 6NT if no good trump fit has been located.

Fourth-suit-forcing
A minimum bid by opener in reply to fourth-suit-forcing may be passed. Any rebid by responder after fourth-suit-forcing commits the partnership to game. A jump in the fourth suit shows a 5–5 pattern and game values (e.g., 1♡:1♠, 2♣:3◇).

Bidding by a passed hand
The 2NT strong raise structure still applies and requires at least four trumps. Jumps to the three-level (e.g., Pass:1♡, 3♣) show a strong five-card suit, a maximum pass and support for opener's major. Opener's 3-Major rebid is a sign-off.

Responder's 2♣ response (e.g., Pass:1♡, 2♣) is the Drury Convention, asking whether opener has a weak third-in-hand opening or a sound opening. Opener rebids 2◇ if sub-minimum. All other rebids promise sound opening values and commit the partnership to game. Pass: 1♡, 2♣ would also deny a spade suit. Other two-level responses are natural (five-card or longer suit) but are not forcing. On borderline hands, prefer 2♣ Drury to the 2NT response which commits the partnership to the three-level.

Partnership Bidding

How should the following hands be bid? West is the dealer on each hand?

WEST	EAST	WEST	EAST
1. ♠ KJ762	1. ♠ 83	7. ♠ A7	7. ♠ KQ4
♡ AQ	♡ K72	♡ AQJ43	♡ 752
◇ Q753	◇ K84	◇ K972	◇ AQ8
♣ J8	♣ KQ742	♣ Q9	♣ AK76
2. ♠ 73	2. ♠ AJ8	8. ♠ AJ862	8. ♠ KQ1095
♡ AQ872	♡ J54	♡ KQ3	♡ A92
◇ KQJ	◇ A62	◇ 74	◇ J65
♣ 642	♣ KQJ3	♣ 962	♣ 84
3. ♠ 6	3. ♠ AQ8	9. ♠ 642	9. ♠ 95
♡ KJ854	♡ A7	♡ K97	♡ AJ8643
◇ KQ863	◇ 752	◇ 74	◇ A2
♣ A4	♣ KQ973	♣ AQJ96	♣ K43
4. ♠ A7652	4. ♠ 83	10. ♠ AQ62	10. ♠ KJ743
♡ KQJ	♡ A983	♡ 76	♡ A9
◇ 754	◇ KJ62	◇ K964	◇ A73
♣ A3	♣ KQ4	♣ Q63	♣ 854
5. ♠ KQJ72	5. ♠ 6	11. ♠ 972	11. ♠ KQJ43
♡ K873	♡ A952	♡ A84	♡ KQ72
◇ A954	◇ K62	◇ Q972	◇ A8
♣ ---	♣ KQ762	♣ KQ3	♣ 62
6. ♠ A97	6. ♠ KQ4	12. ♠ A	12. ♠ KJ752
♡ KJ643	♡ 752	♡ 983	♡ KQ6
◇ KJ42	◇ AQ8	◇ AJ10642	◇ 83
♣ 9	♣ AK76	♣ 762	♣ K43

Chapter 10

The 1NT and 2NT Openings

1NT: 15–17 HCP, balanced shape, no 5-card major. With 5–3–3–2 and a 5-card major, open 1-Major and rebid 1NT (1♡ : 1♠, 1NT) or pass a 1NT response with 15, but with 16–17 rebid 2NT (1♡ : 1♠, 2NT, or 1♠ : 2♣, 2NT).

Responses
2♣ = Stayman. Standard continuations. Responder's suit rebid at the two-level is weak, 2NT invitational, 3♣ a sign-off and other three-level bids are forcing.
Transfers: All two-level responses other than 2♣.
  2♢ = 5+ hearts
  2♡ = 5+ spades
  2♠ = 5+ clubs
  2NT = 5+ diamonds (With a normal raise to 2NT, use 2♣ Stayman and rebid 2NT to show invitational values. With transfers, 2♣ Stayman need not contain a 4-card major if the rebid is 2NT.)
  Responder may be weak or strong for the transfer. Opener will normally just bid the transfer suit (e.g., 1NT : 2♢, 2♡) and if wishing to sign off, responder will simply pass. After a transfer to hearts or spades, responder's 2NT rebid or raise to the three-level is invitational. With a 5-card major and just game values, responder will transfer and rebid 3NT or a new suit (natural and forcing). With a 6-card or longer major and no slam ambitions, responder can transfer and rebid 4-Major.
  Opener must accept the transfer regardless of opener's holding in responder's suit. After a transfer to a major, opener may 'super-accept' (bid the major at the three-level, e.g., 1NT : 2♡, 3♠) with maximum points, support for the major and a doubleton outside. After a transfer to a minor, opener bids the minor shown with ordinary values. With a maximum 1NT and support for the minor including at least the queen, opener super-accepts by bidding the in-between step (e.g., 1NT : 2♠, 2NT or 1NT : 2NT, 3♣). If responder is weak, responder signs off in the minor.

Three-level Responses
3♣ or 3♢ = 6-card minor, invitational values. With game values and a one-suiter, respond 3NT. With other strong hands, use the transfer structure.
3♡ or 3♠ = 5+ major, one-suiter, slam values. With game values only, use the transfer structure.

Partnership Bidding

How should the following hands be bid, using the methods on page 54? West is the dealer on each hand.

	WEST		EAST		WEST		EAST
1.	♠ A742 ♡ K3 ♢ AQ6 ♣ K754	1.	♠ 83 ♡ Q97542 ♢ 942 ♣ 83	7.	♠ AQ32 ♡ QJ8 ♢ AQ54 ♣ J3	7.	♠ 965 ♡ A10542 ♢ KJ3 ♣ 76
2.	♠ J10962 ♡ 82 ♢ 9832 ♣ 84	2.	♠ Q73 ♡ KJ4 ♢ AKJ ♣ K965	8.	♠ K972 ♡ AK62 ♢ A8 ♣ K53	8.	♠ A86543 ♡ 975 ♢ 43 ♣ Q8
3.	♠ K8743 ♡ J986 ♢ 732 ♣ 6	3.	♠ J2 ♡ KQ104 ♢ A1086 ♣ AK5	9.	♠ Q8765 ♡ A8 ♢ QJ10 ♣ Q84	9.	♠ K42 ♡ 932 ♢ AK532 ♣ AJ
4.	♠ AJ42 ♡ KQ63 ♢ 98 ♣ AQJ	4.	♠ 6 ♡ 52 ♢ KQ7643 ♣ 8752	10.	♠ 8743 ♡ KJ4 ♢ K76 ♣ AKQ	10.	♠ KQ1095 ♡ 3 ♢ AJ1054 ♣ 62
5.	♠ 4 ♡ Q83 ♢ 72 ♣ J1097643	5.	♠ AJ93 ♡ K7 ♢ KQ84 ♣ Q82	11.	♠ KQ65 ♡ A953 ♢ A9 ♣ Q76	11.	♠ AJ732 ♡ KQJ4 ♢ 72 ♣ 83
6.	♠ 86 ♡ 642 ♢ AQJ742 ♣ 93	6.	♠ AQ3 ♡ A95 ♢ K86 ♣ A842	12.	♠ AK53 ♡ J98 ♢ AQJ6 ♣ J3	12.	♠ 82 ♡ 752 ♢ 92 ♣ AKQ982

2NT = 21–22 points, and balanced shape.

Responses
3♣ = Stayman. Standard continuations. Opener bids 3◇ with no major or bids a 4-card major (bid 3♡ with both majors). After a 3♡ reply (2NT:3♣, 3♡), responder bids 3NT with four spades and no slam ambitions. Opener can correct to 4♠ with four spades as responder will have a 4-card major to use 3♣ and rebid 3NT. With four spades and slam prospects, responder can bid 3♠ (forcing) over 3♡.

3◇ = Transfer, 5+ hearts
3♡ = Transfer, 5+ spades

These may be used with very weak hands and responder may pass opener's acceptance of the transfer (2NT:3♡, 3♠:Pass). With maximum values, four trumps and a doubleton, opener should super-accept by bidding 4-Major.

Over a simple acceptance by opener (2NT:3◇, 3♡), responder may bid 3NT (game values with a 5-card major), bid 4-Major (sign-off with a 6+ suit) or bid a new suit below game (forcing). A rebid in game is not forcing (e.g., 2NT:3♡, 3♠:4♡ asks opener to choose the better major game). A transfer followed by 4NT is Blackwood, based on responder's suit as trumps (e.g., 2NT:3♡, 3♠:4NT).

Other responses to 2NT
Game bids are to play (e.g., 2NT:4♠ or 2NT:5♣).
2NT:3♠ = Both minors and slam interest.
4♣ or 4◇ = Single-suiter and slam interest. With support, opener cue-bids. Without support, opener bids 4NT. With a long minor and a 4-card major and slam potential, bid 3♣ Stayman first. If no major fit comes to light, continue by bidding your minor at the four level. For example:

2NT:3♣	or	2NT:3♣	In each case responder has missed the
3♡ :3♠		3♠ :4◇	major fit and is now showing at least a
3NT:4♣			5-card minor and slam interest.

Partnership Bidding

How should the following hands be bid, using the methods on page 56? West is the dealer on each hand.

WEST	EAST	WEST	EAST

1. ♠ AK3   1. ♠ Q9852   7. ♠ AJ3   7. ♠ K8
   ♡ KJ8   ♡ Q763   ♡ KQ72   ♡ 4
   ◇ A963   ◇ 74   ◇ A986   ◇ KQ542
   ♣ AK7   ♣ 52   ♣ AK   ♣ Q9873

2. ♠ J108764 2. ♠ K52   8. ♠ AQ86   8. ♠ K3
   ♡ 3   ♡ AKJ4   ♡ AK73   ♡ 84
   ◇ QJ2   ◇ A96   ◇ A7   ◇ KQJ43
   ♣ 943   ♣ AQ8   ♣ A85   ♣ K762

3. ♠ KQJ   3. ♠ 72   9. ♠ 9   9. ♠ QJ6
   ♡ AQ5   ♡ K9643   ♡ 542   ♡ AKQ
   ◇ AJ94   ◇ Q852   ◇ KQ9653   ◇ A84
   ♣ A96   ♣ 72   ♣ AJ6   ♣ KQ93

4. ♠ KQ8   4. ♠ 976532 10. ♠ AKJ2   10. ♠ 83
   ♡ A73   ♡ 862   ♡ AKQ   ♡ J9
   ◇ AK4   ◇ 92   ◇ Q1083   ◇ A65
   ♣ AJ92   ♣ 54   ♣ K6   ♣ AJ8743

5. ♠ 72   5. ♠ A93   11. ♠ KJ862 11. ♠ AQ54
   ♡ 986542   ♡ AK73   ♡ 92   ♡ AK3
   ◇ 93   ◇ AQJ8   ◇ A7   ◇ K954
   ♣ 742   ♣ A9   ♣ 8643   ♣ AQ

6. ♠ AQ7   6. ♠ K9643   12. ♠ KJ762 12. ♠ A53
   ♡ KQ83   ♡ 7   ♡ KQ864   ♡ AJ52
   ◇ A98   ◇ KQ642   ◇ 76   ◇ K92
   ♣ AQ3   ♣ K8   ♣ 4   ♣ AKQ

Opening 2NT when holding a five-card major

The 5-3-3-2 hand of 21-22 points with a five-card major is very difficult to bid. To open with a one bid is unsatisfactory: responder may pass and a game could be missed. To open 2♡ or 2♠ showing an Acol Two is not attractive unless partner is permitted to pass. Since the Acol 2♡/2♠ opening may also be bid on freakish shapes, responder is expected to respond even on hopeless hands in case opener has excellent playing strength. One cannot cater for both these situations.

To open 2NT with this hand-type is the least of evils: the strength and shape are described accurately and responder is permitted to pass with a worthless hand. The drawback is that with standard methods, the partnership may play in 3NT (or 6NT) when a superior contract exists in a 5-3 major fit. You should not miss a 5-4 major fit, as responder should use 3♣ Stayman with a four-card major.

It is possible to adapt the responses to 3♣ Stayman to enable opener to show a 5-card major and allow responder to check whether a 4-4 major fit exists.

5-Card major Stayman
AFTER 2NT : 3♣ —
3♢ = No 5-card major, but a 4-card major is held
3♡ or 3♠ = 5-card major
3NT = No 4-card major.

AFTER 3♢:
With no four-card major, responder bids 3NT or 4♣ (see below). With a four-card major, responder bids 3♡ or 3♠, the major which responder does NOT hold. The idea is to allow opener to be declarer if a major fit exists. Opener bids 3NT if holding the major responder has denied or bids 4-Major if holding the major responder has promised.
2NT : 3♣, 3♢ : 4♢ shows responder has both majors. Opener bids the major suit held. Again opener is declarer.
2NT : 3♣, 3♢ : 4♣ asks for a 4-card minor. Opener bids 4♢ with diamonds, 4♡ or 4♠ as a cue bid with a club suit and 4NT with no 4-card minor.
2NT : 3♣, 3NT : 4♣ also asks for opener's minor. 4♢ shows diamonds and 4♡/4♠ are cue bids with a club suit.

Partnership Bidding

How should the following hands be bid, using the methods on page 58? West is the dealer on each hand.

WEST	EAST	WEST	EAST
1. ♠ AQ864 ♡ KQ7 ◇ A8 ♣ AQ9	1. ♠ KJ2 ♡ J943 ◇ 96 ♣ 10852	7. ♠ AJ62 ♡ 987 ◇ Q4 ♣ 8632	7. ♠ KQ73 ♡ K52 ◇ KJ2 ♣ AKQ
2. ♠ AQ864 ♡ KQ7 ◇ A8 ♣ AO9	2. ♠ 93 ♡ J943 ◇ KJ2 ♣ 10865	8. ♠ AJ85 ♡ AQ ◇ AK3 ♣ A754	8. ♠ 94 ♡ J632 ◇ Q94 ♣ O862
3. ♠ Q763 ♡ J742 ◇ A4 ♣ 962	3. ♠ K2 ♡ AK965 ◇ KQ7 ♣ AQ5	9. ♠ Q872 ♡ Q954 ◇ K4 ♣ 762	9. ♠ AK43 ♡ K3 ◇ AJ52 ♣ AQ3
4. ♠ Q763 ♡ J762 ◇ 873 ♣ K4	4. ♠ K2 ♡ KQ4 ◇ AK965 ♣ AQ5	10. ♠ A873 ♡ AQJ3 ◇ K7 ♣ AK4	10. ♠ K642 ♡ K642 ◇ 86 ♣ 532
5. ♠ J72 ♡ 83 ◇ A984 ♣ J1062	5. ♠ KQ643 ♡ A97 ◇ KQ ♣ AK3	11. ♠ AJ942 ♡ J864 ◇ A3 ♣ 74	11. ♠ K8 ♡ AK92 ◇ KJ54 ♣ AK2
6. ♠ KQ82 ♡ K62 ◇ A5 ♣ AKQ2	6. ♠ 76 ♡ AJ875 ◇ 982 ♣ 974	12. ♠ A75 ♡ AK42 ◇ K9 ♣ AKJ3	12. ♠ K862 ♡ Q9753 ◇ AQ7 ♣ 6

Chapter 11

The One Club and One Diamond Openings

The opening bids are chosen as in standard methods (*see* Chapter 4). The responding structure follows the same pattern as for the major suit openings.

1♣:2♣ or 1◇:2◇ shows support and 6–9 points. Raising a minor denies a 4-card major.

1♣:3♣ or 1◇:3◇ shows support, 6–9 points and 8 losers. The hand will be shapely with no 4-card major. These raises are essentially pre-emptive. The loser count will help opener to decide whether a sacrifice will be acceptable if the opponents do bid a major suit game.

Losing Trick Count
Add your losers to the losers shown by partner's bid. Deduct the total from 24. The answer is the number of tricks your side will probably win with normal breaks and half your finesses working.

Stronger hands with support for opener's minor and no 4-card major are shown via 2NT.

1♣:2NT or 1◇:2NT shows 10 HCP or more, support for opener's minor and no 4-card major. The hand need not be balanced. All strong hands with support and no major travel through 2NT.

1♣:3NT or 1◇:3NT shows 15–17 points, a 4-3-3-3 with no 4-card major and stoppers in the unbid suits. Opener decides whether to push on to a slam. With the same strength and pattern and no stopper in one of the unbid suits, either use 2NT or bid the other minor (new-suit-forcing).

The priorities in responding remain the same:
- Change suit (especially if holding a major)
- Support opener's minor
- Bid 1NT (6–9 points) or 3NT if the hand fits.
When changing suit, bid longest suit first, the higher of two 5-card suits and up-the-line with 4-card suits.

Exercise

A. Partner has opened One Club. What is your response on these hands?

1. ♠ 72
♡ 86
♢ K863
♣ QJ975

2. ♠ KJ7
♡ AQ2
♢ KQ7
♣ J832

3. ♠ KJ73
♡ AQ2
♢ KQ7
♣ J83

4. ♠ A73
♡ 6
♢ 985
♣ Q76432

5. ♠ K9
♡ AJ8
♢ A83
♣ Q9742

6. ♠ 962
♡ 86
♢ K97
♣ AK832

B. Partner has opened One Diamond. What is your response on these hands?

1. ♠ KJ7
♡ 843
♢ KQ72
♣ Q82

2. ♠ KQ7
♡ 9843
♢ KQ72
♣ Q8

3. ♠ KQ7
♡ A84
♢ KQ7
♣ Q862

4. ♠ 7
♡ A83
♢ Q983
♣ J10764

5. ♠ 7
♡ AK3
♢ Q983
♣ J10764

6. ♠ 762
♡ A8
♢ AKJ8
♣ QJ32

OPENER'S REBID

AFTER 1♣:1◇ or after a major suit response, opener's priorities remain the same as in standard methods (*see* page 34). The Barrier Principle and the Skip-over Principle apply.

AFTER 1♣:2♣ or 1◇:2◇
Change of suit is forcing (16 points or more), 2NT is invitational. A jump-shift is natural and is forcing to game.

AFTER 1♣:3♣ or 1◇:3◇
Responder is weak, so that opener will pass with most ordinary openings. A rebid of a major at the three-level will be a stopper bid, showing a stopper in the suit bid and looking for 3NT. Stoppers are shown up-the-line and bypassing a suit denies a stopper in that suit. For example, 1♣:3♣, 3♡ shows a stopper in hearts and denies a stopper in diamonds. Responder can show a stopper in return or bid 3NT if holding a stopper in the danger suit (a suit where opener has denied a stopper). With no stopper in the danger suit, responder returns to the agreed minor. Bid 4-minor with two or more losers in the danger suit and 5-minor with a singleton in the danger suit. In the odd case where you have a void in the danger suit, bid the danger suit at the four-level. For example, 1◇:3◇, 3♠:4♡ . . . 3♠ showed a spade stopper and expressed concern about hearts. 4♡ indicated a void in hearts. It clearly cannot be natural as 1◇:3◇ denied a major.

AFTER 1♣:2NT or 1◇:2NT
Responder has at least 10 points and support for opener's minor. With most 12–14 point hands, opener will bid 3-minor, prepared to play there opposite about 10–11 points. With more than that, responder will bid on.

Other rebids by opener at the three-level are stopper-showing and show game values. Stoppers are shown up-the-line and the stopper-showing structure follows the same lines as above.

If opener has shown a minimum by bidding 3-minor, responder will bid on with game prospects. A bid at the three-level will start stopper-showing. Raising the minor to the four-level is forcing, indicates slam potential and asks opener to start cue-bidding.

Exercise

A. WEST   EAST

1♣   2♣   What action should West now take on these
?   hands?

1. ♠ KQ7   2. ♠ AJ8   3. ♠ AJ82
    ♡ A763   ♡ KJ72   ♡ 96
    ◇ Q8   ◇ AK   ◇ AK4
    ♣ Q975   ♣ K985   ♣ AQJ6

4. ♠ A7   5. ♠ A3   6. ♠ AQ3
    ♡ K9   ♡ K4   ♡ KQ72
    ◇ KQ43   ◇ A76   ◇ 8
    ♣ KJ872   ♣ AQ9832   ♣ AJ864

B. WEST   EAST

1♣   3♣
?   What should West do next on these hands?

1. ♠ KQ3   2. ♠ A7   3. ♠ AJ8
    ♡ A974   ♡ AK9   ♡ KQJ2
    ◇ K5   ◇ 74   ◇ AK4
    ♣ Q862   ♣ AQ8632   ♣ Q72

C. WEST   EAST

1◇   2NT   What action should West take next on these
?   hands?

1. ♠ A864   2. ♠ KJ102   3. ♠ AK83
    ♡ A7   ♡ AQ10   ♡ 73
    ◇ K973   ◇ 8763   ◇ AKJ86
    ♣ Q64   ♣ A9   ♣ 92

OTHER REBIDS BY RESPONDER

The standard principles for responder's rebid apply (*see* page 36). In addition, the 2♣ Game Try rebid is used after opener's one-level rebid. Thus:

1♣:1♠, 1NT:2♣
1♣:1♡, 1NT:2♣
1♣:1◇, 1NT:2♣

In each case, the 2♣ bid is artificial and responder is making a game try. With a weak hand with clubs, pass 1NT or jump to 3♣ which is not encouraging. With a game force, responder can bid a suit other than clubs at the three-level or bid 2NT over 1NT (game force, artificial).

1◇:1♡, 1NT:2♣
1◇:1♠, 1NT:2♣

Again 2♣ is the artificial game try. 2NT by responder is also a game force and all jumps to the three-level (including 3♣) are natural and forcing to game. A jump to the three-level in a new suit shows at least a 5–5 pattern (e.g., 1◇:1♠, 1NT:3♣). With a 5–4 shape, use 2NT.

1♣:1◇, 1♡:2♣
1♣:1◇, 1♠:2♣
1♣:1♡, 1♠:2♣

Again 2♣ is the artificial game try. With a weak hand with clubs, jump to 3♣. 2NT in each of these auctions is natural and limited, as fourth-suit-forcing is available. After 1♣:1◇, 1♡ responder's 1♠ is natural and forcing (6 points up) and 2♠ is artificial and becomes fourth-suit-forcing, denying four spades.

1◇:1♡, 1♠:2♣

Here 2♣ is fourth-suit-forcing and 2NT by responder would be natural and limited (about 11–12 points). Jumps to the three-level would also be natural and invitational only except for 1◇:1♡, 1♠:3♣ (jump in the fourth suit shows a game-force 5–5 pattern). Other game-going hands travel through 2♣ fourth suit.

OPENER'S REPLY TO THE 2♣ GAME TRY

The expectancy for 2♣ is 11–12 points. A particularly strong 10 count will do. Opener bids as follows:

2◇ = Artificial minimum, 11–13 points. Further bidding is natural, seeking the best partscore.

All others show 14 points or more and create a game-forcing auction. The bidding is natural until the best contract is found.

Partnership Bidding

How should the following hands be bid, using the methods on page 64? West is the dealer on each hand.

WEST	EAST	WEST	EAST
1. ♣ KQ72	1. ♣ 963	7. ♣ KQ7	7. ♣ 932
♡ A6	♡ K972	♡ J9	♡ AQ653
◇ K983	◇ A52	◇ A742	◇ KJ
♣ 864	♣ KJ7	♣ K1096	♣ 872
2. ♠ KQ72	2. ♠ A3	8. ♠ KQJ	8. ♠ 932
♡ A63	♡ K9742	♡ K83	♡ AQ65
◇ K983	◇ AJ2	◇ A962	◇ KJ
♣ 86	♣ J54	♣ J107	♣ Q863
3. ♠ KQ	3. ♠ J742	9. ♠ AJ2	9. ♠ KQ764
♡ A98	♡ K76	♡ KQ6	♡ J743
◇ 762	◇ A43	◇ K83	◇ A9
♣ AJ652	♣ K107	♣ J842	♣ 63
4. ♠ Q65	4. ♠ J7	10. ♠ A7	10. ♠ K6
♡ A98	♡ KQ3	♡ KQ93	♡ A542
◇ A72	◇ K9843	◇ K76	◇ QJ82
♣ K862	♣ Q74	♣ 8642	♣ J53
5. ♠ Q8	5. ♠ AJ762	11. ♠ KQ86	11. ♠ J3
♡ A752	♡ KQJ3	♡ 64	♡ KQJ53
◇ A53	◇ K4	◇ AQJ3	◇ 2
♣ K984	♣ 62	♣ 754	♣ AK632
6. ♠ Q84	6. ♠ AJ762	12. ♠ A83	12. ♠ KQ742
♡ K86	♡ A9532	♡ KJ4	♡ A73
◇ K83	◇ AJ	◇ AJ63	◇ KQ2
♣ KQ75	♣ 8	♣ 932	♣ 86

COMPETITIVE BIDDING

1. They double your opening bid.

All responses retain the normal meaning including 2NT.

Redouble = 10 HCP or more and a desire to play for penalties. The hand type suitable for a redouble is one which is short in opener's suit and has a strong 4-card or longer holding in at least two of the other suits. Responder is thus able to double at least two suits for penalties. With other hand types, take your normal responding action.

After a redouble, all doubles are for penalties.

2. They overcall in a suit at the one-level or two-level.

Change of suit is forcing. A jump to 2NT retains its meaning but promises a stopper in their suit. Bidding their suit at the two-level, for example, 1♣:(1♡):2♡ shows the same values as the 2NT response but no stopper in their suit. It may be vital for the hand with the stopper in their suit to be the declarer in no-trumps.

Negative Doubles

The double of a suit overcall at the one-level or two-level is for takeout. The standard approach is for the double to promise 6 points or more (normal responding values) and at least four cards in any unbid major. 1♣:(1◇):Double or 1◇:(2♣): Double promises at least 4–4 in the majors.

1♡:(1♠):Double	Where both majors have been bid, the
1♡:(2♠):Double	double shows at least 4–4 in the minors. This
1♠:(2♡):Double	is very convenient, particularly for a weak
	responding hand which otherwise finds it
	virtually impossible to reveal this hand type.
1♣:(1♡):Double	The standard approach is that double of one
1◇:(1♡):Double	major promises four cards in the other
	major. Thus, here double shows four spades
	and 1♠ would show five spades. Major over
	major promises five. This is a useful distinc-
	tion.

However, many experts play that 1♠ over a 1♡ overcall promises only four cards, as though there had been no interference. The double over 1♡ is used to show minor suit values but too weak to bid at the two-level. You and partner need to decide which way you will play the double of 1♡.

Your partnership may also decide to play negative doubles at the three-level or four-level.

Partnership Bidding

How should the following hands be bid, using the methods on page 66? West is the dealer on each hand. There is no North–South bidding other than that given.

WEST		EAST		WEST		EAST	
1.	N doubles	1.	N doubles	5.	N bids 1♠	5.	N bids 1♠
	S bids 2♣		S bids 2♣		S bids 2♠		S bids 2♠
	♠ KJ8		♠ A1073		♠ J7		♠ 962
	♡ A973		♡ K85		♡ KO63		♡ A874
	◇ AJ82		◇ 6		◇ Q43		◇ AJ109
	♣ 86		♣ K10742		♣ AJ82		♣ K3
2.	N bids 1♠	2.	N bids 1♠	6.	N bids 1♠	6.	N bids 1♠
	♠ AJ6		♠ 87		♠ AQ7		♠ 83
	♡ K762		♡ A93		♡ K9		♡ A752
	◇ KQ83		◇ AJ72		◇ K8642		◇ A95
	♣ 42		♣ KQ63		♣ 832		♣ AJ76
3.	N bids 1♠	3.	N bids 1♠	7.	N bids 2♣	7.	N bids 2♣
	♠ 763		♠ AQ2		♠ 7		♠ AJ53
	♡ KQJ		♡ A95		♡ 62		♡ KQ43
	◇ AJ74		◇ 108632		◇ AQJ65		◇ 874
	♣ Q72		♣ 65		♣ KQ974		♣ 62
4.	N bids 1♡	4.	N bids 1♡	8.	N bids 2♣	8.	N bids 2♣
	♠ A7		♠ KJ6		♠ A63		♠ J742
	♡ 62		♡ 8743		♡ KQJ		♡ A853
	◇ AQ9643		◇ KJ75		◇ AKQ3		◇ 92
	♣ AQJ		♣ K8		♣ 742		♣ QJ6

Chapter 12

Suit Openings at the Two Level

The suit openings at the two level cater for strong hands just below game-force values (Acol Twos), game-forcing hands, balanced hands with 23 HCP or stronger and weak twos in the majors. 2♡ and 2♠ show Acol Twos, 2♣ caters·for all the game force hands including balanced hands of 25 HCP or more. All the others are included in the Multi 2◇ opening (weak two in a major OR Acol Two in a minor OR a balanced hand of 23–24 points).

THE 2♣ OPENING

Open 2♣ if you have:
- Any balanced hand with 25 HCP or more
- Any unbalanced hand with 23 HCP or more
- Any hand below 23 HCP with 3 losers or better with a long major suit or two losers or better with a long minor suit.

Responses

2◇ = Negative, 0–7 points, any shape. A 7-point hand including 1½ quick tricks should give a positive response. An ace and a king or a suit headed by A-Q counts as 1½ quick tricks. The function of the negative response is to indicate a hand without slam potential if opener has no better than a ten-trick hand.

Bidding after 2◇ is natural and leads to game. The 2♣:2◇, 2NT sequence shows 25 points or more and is forcing. Responder bids as though responding to a 2NT opening (3♣ Stayman, transfers and so on – *see* page 56).

All other responses = positive, 8 points or more (or 7 points with 1½ quick tricks). The positive responses are natural. A major suit response may be a four-card suit, 2NT is balanced and denies a major and 3♣ or 3◇ shows at least a five-card suit. Any positive response will usually lead to a slam.

The jump responses (2♣:3♡/3♠/4♣/4◇) show a powerful suit, playable opposite a singleton.

Suit Quality Test

Add the number of cards in your long suit to the number of honour cards in your long suit. For example, K-Q-8-6-4-2 has a suit quality of 8 (Length 6 + Honours 2), while Q-9-5-3-2 has a suit quality of six (Length 5 + Honours 1).

RULE-OF-10: If Length + Honours = 10, you can insist on your suit as trumps even if partner does not have support. For example, holdings such as A-Q-J-x-x-x or K-Q-J-10-x-x fulfil the Rule-of-10.

Partnership Bidding

How should the following hands be bid, using the methods on page 68? West is the dealer on each hand.

	WEST		EAST		WEST		EAST
1.	♠ 7643	1.	♠ KQJ10	7.	♠ K972	7.	♠ A6
	♡ 63		♡ A82		♡ A7		♡ KQ53
	◇ 862		◇ AKQ		◇ 9843		◇ AKQJ72
	♣ 8732		♣ AK5		♣ Q65		♣ A
2.	♠ AQJ	2.	♠ 10653	8.	♠ A9	8.	♠ K5
	♡ KQJ6		♡ 87		♡ 75		♡ AQJ103
	◇ AK4		◇ Q72		◇ K9762		◇ AQ84
	♣ AQ3		♣ 9852		♣ 7432		♣ AK
3.	♠ J754	3.	♠ KQ	9.	♠ A	9.	♠ 864
	♡ Q6432		♡ AK5		♡ K72		♡ AQJ1063
	◇ 832		◇ AK97		◇ AKQJ3		◇ 64
	♣ 6		♣ AQ105		♣ AQJ2		♣ 74
4.	♠ KQJ	4.	♠ 984	10.	♠ 62	10.	♠ KQJ1075
	♡ AKQ5		♡ 632		♡ AKQ		♡ 63
	◇ AKJ		◇ Q74		◇ AK9743		◇ 5
	♣ AQ10		♣ K853		♣ AK		♣ J862
5.	♠ 976542	5.	♠ KQ3	11.	♠ 52	11.	♠ KQJ8763
	♡ 83		♡ AKQ6		♡ 9874		♡ AK
	◇ 954		◇ AK3		◇ QJ4		◇ A8
	♣ J3		♣ AK6		♣ J753		♣ KQ
6.	♠ KQ	6.	♠ 98643	12.	♠ AKQ974	12.	♠ 8632
	♡ AJ86		♡ 53		♡ KQJ		♡ A752
	◇ AKQ		◇ 4		◇ A		◇ 9762
	♣ AK53		♣ Q7642		♣ A73		♣ 4

THE 2♡ AND 2♠ OPENINGS

These should contain either 21–22 HCP with at least a five-card suit or more than eight playing tricks.

A hand with just eight playing tricks or less should be opened with a one bid. If you have eight tricks, partner will need to provide two tricks for you to make 4♡ or 4♠. If partner has the two tricks required (two aces, an ace and a king, even two kings) partner has enough to respond to a one-opening. You therefore do not need to open two on such a hand. If partner passes your one-opening, it is highly unlikely you will miss a game.

The 2♡ and 2♠ openings are used for hands where one trick with partner may be enough for a game. Perhaps one ace, or a useful king, and game will be a good bet. Yet these are holdings where partner would pass your one opening. Open 2♡ or 2♠ with –

21–22 HCP and a 5-card major
19–20 HCP and a 6-card major
17–18 HCP and a 7-card major
Weaker hands with 8½ to 9½ playing tricks
With ten playing tricks (3 losers) and a long major, open 2♣.

Responding to 2♡ or 2♠
These bids are forcing for one round. With a poor hand, bid 2NT (0–7 points). The jump raise to game shows support and two kings but no aces. With good support and at least one ace, raise opener's major to the three-level, suggesting slam possibilities and asking opener to start cue bidding.

Any bid other than 2NT is natural, shows 8 points or more (a good 7 will do) and commits the partnership to game. A jump response in a new suit (2♡ : 3♠/4♣/4♢ or 2♠ : 4♣/4♢/4♡) is a splinter, showing 4+ support, a singleton or void in the suit bid and a positive response. Opener is asked to assess the usefulness of the short suit for slam purposes.

After 2NT, any rebid by opener is droppable except for:

● A jump to 4♣ or 4♢, showing a powerful two-suiter and insisting on game.

● The sequence 2♡ : 2NT, 3♠ is also forcing and shows a 6–5 pattern.

Responder may, of course, bid on even where opener's rebid is droppable. All further bidding is natural.

Exercise

A. What is your opening bid on each of these hands?

1. ♠ KQJ964
   ♡ AKJ
   ◇ AQ
   ♣ 72

2. ♠ KQJ964
   ♡ AKJ
   ◇ AQ
   ♣ A2

3. ♠ 6
   ♡ AQJ972
   ◇ AKJ1063
   ♣ —

4. ♠ AQJ93
   ♡ KQJ874
   ◇ A
   ♣ 3

5. ♠ AQ932
   ♡ KQJ87
   ◇ AJ
   ♣ 6

6. ♠ AKJ97642
   ♡ AK
   ◇ 53
   ♣ 4

B. Partner opens 2♡. What is your response?

1. ♠ J74
   ♡ 98
   ◇ J653
   ♣ 7532

2. ♠ K65
   ♡ K843
   ◇ 98
   ♣ 6542

3. ♠ A87
   ♡ K963
   ◇ K2
   ♣ 6532

C. Partner opens 2♠. What is your response?

1. ♠ 63
   ♡ 7
   ◇ AQJ64
   ♣ KJ872

2. ♠ Q962
   ♡ 7632
   ◇ AK87
   ♣ 7

3. ♠ Q974
   ♡ 76
   ◇ Q632
   ♣ 862

THE MULTI-TWO DIAMOND OPENING

This caters for –
* A weak two in either major, *OR*
* An Acol Two in either minor, *OR*
* A balanced hand of 23–24 HCP

Responses
Responder assumes a weak two is held and bids accordingly:

2♡ = Pass if you have a weak two in hearts, otherwise bid on.

2♠ = Pass if you have a weak two in spades, otherwise bid on. The 2♠ response shows enough to invite game opposite a weak two in hearts. If weaker than that, respond 2♡.

2NT = Strong enquiry, enough for a game invitation opposite a weak two (16 HCP or more with no major fit, about 3½ tricks or more with a major suit fit).

3♣/3♢ = Strong and natural, forcing for one round.

3♡/3♠ = Pre-emptive with support for both majors.

Opener's Rebid
After 2♢:2♡
* Pass with a weak two in hearts.
* Bid 2♠ with a weak two in spades. Responder continues as after a standard weak 2♠ opening (*see* Chapter 7).
* Bid 2NT with 23–24 balanced. Responder continues as after a 2NT opening (*see* pages 56–58).
* Bid 3♣ or 3♢ to show an Acol two in the suit bid.
* Bid 3NT to show nine playing tricks including A-K-Q-x-x-x-x or better in one of the minors and at least two stoppers outside.

After 2♢:2♠
* Pass with a weak two in spades.
* Bid 3♡ with a minimum weak 2♡ and 4♡ with a maximum 2♡.
* Bid 2NT with 23–24 balanced.
* Bid 3♣ or 3♢ or 3NT as above with an Acol Two in a minor.

After 2♢:2NT
* Bid 3♣ with a good weak two in hearts.
* Bid 3♢ with a good weak two in spades.
* Bid 3♡ or 3♠ with a minimum weak two with only one top honour in your long major.
* Bid 3NT with A-K-Q-x-x-x in your major.

- Bid 4♣ or 4◇ with an Acol Two in the suit bid. You will reach a slam given the strength of the 2NT response.
- Bid 4♡ or 4♠ with a maximum weak two and a Rule-of-10 suit.
- Bid 4NT with 23–24 balanced. Opposite a 2NT response, the partnership will reach at least 6NT.

Partnership Bidding

How should the following hands be bid, using the methods on page 72? West is the dealer on each hand.

	WEST		EAST		WEST		EAST
1.	♠ A7 ♡ KQ9843 ◇ 75 ♣ 862	1.	♠ KJ43 ♡ 62 ◇ A842 ♣ 753	7.	♠ A107642 ♡ 64 ◇ QJ2 ♣ 98	7.	♠ KQ8 ♡ AK3 ◇ K985 ♣ AQ6
2.	♠ AKQ763 ♡ 74 ◇ 872 ♣ 98	2.	♠ J2 ♡ A65 ◇ A964 ♣ A754	8.	♠ QJ9862 ♡ 74 ◇ A73 ♣ 54	8.	♠ 73 ♡ AK963 ◇ QJ654 ♣ 3
3.	♠ AKQ763 ♡ 74 ◇ 872 ♣ 98	3.	♠ J2 ♡ J83 ◇ AK4 ♣ 76532	9.	♠ AJ7 ♡ KQ3 ◇ AK4 ♣ KQJ3	9.	♠ K982 ♡ AJ42 ◇ Q9 ♣ A102
4.	♠ KQJ4 ♡ AK ◇ KQ98 ♣ KQ5	4.	♠ 732 ♡ 865 ◇ 7432 ♣ J62	10.	♠ AK2 ♡ 5 ◇ AKQJ762 ♣ 82	10.	♠ 98 ♡ AQ83 ◇ 954 ♣ AQ65
5.	♠ Q974 ♡ 82 ◇ K74 ♣ 8632	5.	♠ AJ52 ♡ A3 ◇ AQ9 ♣ AKJ4	11.	♠ AQJ1074 ♡ 8 ◇ Q93 ♣ J62	11.	♠ 3 ♡ AJ74 ◇ AK52 ♣ KQ97
6.	♠ K72 ♡ K9 ◇ 87632 ♣ J75	6.	♠ 9 ♡ AQ ◇ QJ4 ♣ AKQ8632	12.	♠ J3 ♡ AQ8754 ◇ Q97 ♣ 62	12.	♠ AQ9 ♡ 3 ◇ AK62 ♣ KQJ84

AFTER 2◇:2NT, 3♣ or 2◇:2NT, 3◇

A bid of 3♡ over 3♣ or 3♠ over 3◇ is a sign-off. Any game bid is to play.

If responder needs more information about the strength of the weak two, responder bids the next suit up (3◇ over 3♣ and 3♡ over 3◇). Opener then shows the hand strength in steps (memory guide:2–2–1) as follows:

Step 1 = 2 top honours, minimum points. This will be opener's major in each case, so that responder can pass without enough for game opposite minimum points.

Step 2 = 2 top honours, maximum points.

Step 3 = 1 top honour, maximum points.

A new suit is now a cue bid with opener's suit set as trumps.

Where responder has bid 2NT and bids a new suit over opener's reply, the bid is natural and forcing. For example, in 2◇:2NT, 3♣:3♠, responder is showing a spade suit (six-card suit or powerful five-card suit) which opener should raise with a doubleton, or better.

AFTER 2◇:3♣ or 2◇:3◇

These show a long suit, a strong hand and are forcing. They are not common, as responder will usually use 2NT with a strong hand.

With one of the strong varieties, opener will bid 4NT and reach some slam. With a weak two in a major, opener bids the major at the three-level without support for responder and at the four-level with support for responder as well.

Where opener shows the major at the three-level, responder's rebid of the minor is droppable. A change of suit, however, is forcing. For example, 2◇:3◇, 3♡:3♠ is forcing. Responder is likely to have a strong 6–5 pattern.

AFTER 2◇:3♡ or 2◇:3♠

If opener has the major suit bid, opener will pass. Responder's action is primarily pre-emptive. With a weak two in the other major, opener bids that major. With the strong balanced hand, opener will bid 3NT and with an Acol Two in a minor, opener will bid the minor at the four level. Responder will have taken these possibilities into account when choosing the 3♡ or 3♠ response.

Partnership Bidding

How should the following hands be bid, using the methods on page 74? West is the dealer on each hand.

WEST	EAST	WEST	EAST
1. ♠ A ♡ K86432 ◇ Q72 ♣ 864	1. ♠ J10764 ♡ 975 ◇ K8 ♣ 753	7. ♠ 107 ♡ KQJ984 ◇ 7 ♣ Q743	7. ♠ A52 ♡ 7 ◇ AKJ1063 ♣ AK5
2. ♠ AK8643 ♡ 75 ◇ 86 ♣ 542	2. ♠ J7 ♡ AK9 ◇ KQ74 ♣ KJ63	8. ♠ AJ10754 ♡ 62 ◇ Q7 ♣ 832	8. ♠ — ♡ AJ98 ◇ AK2 ♣ KQJ1076
3. ♠ 72 ♡ AQ10642 ◇ 85 ♣ 832	3. ♠ A64 ♡ K93 ◇ A932 ♣ A76	9. ♠ AQJ754 ♡ 762 ◇ 9 ♣ 642	9. ♠ K93 ♡ 8 ◇ AKQ8762 ♣ A3
4. ♠ KQ9753 ♡ 6 ◇ A93 ♣ 874	4. ♠ A62 ♡ A95 ◇ K8 ♣ AKQ62	10. ♠ KQJ ♡ AJ76 ◇ K93 ♣ AKQ	10. ♠ A ♡ K3 ◇ AQJ8752 ♣ 642
5. ♠ 83 ♡ AQJ652 ◇ 98 ♣ J93	5. ♠ AKJ764 ♡ 9 ◇ KQJ ♣ A76	11. ♠ 7 ♡ AK2 ◇ 98 ♣ AKQJ762	11. ♠ A532 ♡ 7 ◇ AKJ7643 ♣ 5
6. ♠ 6 ♡ AQJ965 ◇ 952 ♣ Q74	6. ♠ A973 ♡ K842 ◇ KQJ ♣ AK	12. ♠ A95 ♡ A8 ◇ AKJ7 ♣ AKJ5	12. ♠ J107 ♡ Q97543 ◇ 6 ♣ 832

Chapter 13

Slam Bidding

While simple Blackwood may be adequate for many hands, Roman Key Card Blackwood does a far better job as it locates not only the aces but also the king and queen of trumps.

Answers to 4NT Roman Key Card Blackwood:

    5♣ = 0 or 3 key cards
    5◇ = 1 or 4 key cards
    5♡ = 2 key cards, no trump queen
    5♠ = 2 key cards plus the trump queen
    5NT = 5 key cards, no trump queen
    6♣ = 5 key cards plus the trump queen

There are five key cards, the four aces and the king of trumps. The trump suit is the agreed suit. If no suit has been agreed yet, 4NT sets the last mentioned suit as trumps.

The 5NT and 6♣ replies almost never occur in practice but if they do, partner should not need any other information.

After a reply of 5♣ or 5◇, the trump queen has not been shown or denied. To ask for the trump queen, bid the cheapest non-trump suit, asking 'Do you have the trump queen?' Partner bids Step 1 to say No, Step 2 to say Yes.

With the replies of 5♣ and 5◇, the number of key cards shown is ambiguous. Most of the time, the 4NT asker will be able to tell from the key cards held or from the bidding, the number that is shown by 5♣ or 5◇. If a situation arises where you genuinely cannot tell which it is, assume it is the lower number and sign off in the agreed trump suit. Partner will then –

Pass with the lower number of key cards.

Bid Step 1 with the higher number of key cards but no trump queen.

Bid Step 2 with the higher number of key cards and the trump queen as well.

After the answer to 4NT or the answer to the trump queen ask, a bid of 5NT asks for kings outside the trump suit. The answers are as for standard Blackwood (6♣ = 0, 6◇ = 1, 6♡ = 2, 6♠ = 3).

After the answer to 4NT or the trump queen ask, a suit bid other than the trump suit asks for control in that suit other than the ace (which is known from the answer to 4NT). Replies are Step 1 = no control, step 2 = Q, step 3 = singleton (if possible), step 4 = K, step 5 = void (if possible), step 6 = K + Q.

Partnership Bidding

How should the following hands be bid, using Roman Key Card Blackwood as described on page 76? West is the dealer on each hand.

	WEST		EAST		WEST		EAST
1.	♠ AK9765	1.	♠ 8432	7.	♠ A964	7.	♠ KJ1073
	♡ 64		♡ A9		♡ AQ		♡ 5
	◇ 73		◇ AKQJ8		◇ 73		◇ AKQ62
	♣ 643		♣ AK		♣ Q9842		♣ AK
2.	♠ 85	2.	♠ AK2	8.	♠ AQ64	8.	♠ KJ1073
	♡ KQJ642		♡ 9753		♡ A3		♡ 5
	◇ J87		◇ A6		◇ 73		◇ AKQ62
	♣ 53		♣ AKQJ		♣ Q9842		♣ AK
3.	♠ AKQJ	3.	♠ 94	9.	♠ K874	9.	♠ AJ1062
	♡ AQJ72		♡ 8643		♡ AJ		♡ Q
	◇ AKQ		◇ 75		◇ AKJ62		◇ 85
	♣ 7		♣ KQ632		♣ 43		♣ AKQ65
4.	♠ AKQJ	4.	♠ 94	10.	♠ KQ74	10.	♠ AJ1062
	♡ AQJ72		♡ K643		♡ A8		♡ Q
	◇ AKQ		◇ 75		◇ AK962		◇ 85
	♣ 7		♣ Q9632		♣ 43		♣ AKQ65
5.	♠ 76	5.	♠ AKQJ	11.	♠ KQJ	11.	♠ 3
	♡ 9843		♡ AQJ72		♡ QJ73		♡ A10952
	◇ 54		◇ AKQ		◇ 2		◇ KQJ53
	♣ AKJ92		♣ 3		♣ AQ642		♣ KJ
6.	♠ 76	6.	♠ AKQJ	12.	♠ A62	12.	♠ 3
	♡ K843		♡ AQJ72		♡ K873		♡ A10952
	◇ 54		◇ AKQ		◇ A		◇ KQJ53
	♣ AJ982		♣ 3		♣ A8642		♣ KJ

Chapter 14

Pre-emptive Openings

The pre-emptive openings from 3♣ upward can follow the traditional methods set out in Chapter 8. Over a pre-empt, change of suit below game is forcing. Opener should support responder's suit with a doubleton or better.

After a three-level pre-empt, it is often awkward to explore slam using 4NT. After a 3♣ pre-empt, the answer may take you beyond 5♣ when 5♣ is the limit. Over a major pre-empt, the five-level may not be safe if partner has insufficient key cards.

A sound approach is to use a cheaper ace-asking mechanism as follows:

Over 3♦, 3♡ or 3♠, 4♣ is used as Blackwood (*see* Chapter 13).

Over 3♣, a response of 4♦ is Blackwood.

In each case, a reply showing insufficient key cards for a slam will leave the partnership comfortably placed at game-level.

Pre-empts at the Four-Level

Another worthwhile scheme for pre-empts at the four-level allows opener to distinguish between strong pre-empts in a major and shaded pre-empts in a major. In this approach –

4♣ = Strong pre-empt of 4♡

4♦ = Strong pre-empt of 4♠

4♡ and 4♠ = Weaker pre-empts

The 4♣ and 4♦ openings show eight playing tricks. Opener will have a suit whose quality satisfies the Rule-of-10 (*see* page 69) and either eight playing tricks in the trump suit itself or seven playing tricks in the trump suit with an outside winner.

3NT = Minor suit pre-empt at the four-level. Thus, 3NT shows a standard opening of 4♣ or 4♦. The difference between this and the gambling 3NT is that the minor suit need not be solid. Responder may pass 3NT or bid 4♡ or 4♠ to play. If responder bids a minor, opener passes if holding that minor, otherwise bids the other minor.

The 4NT opening can also be used to show a specific holding in a minor suit pre-empt. Thus:

4NT = 5-level minor suit pre-empt with a no-loser suit (such as A-K-Q-x-x-x-x-x or better).

5♣ or 5◇ = Pre-empt with a weaker suit.

This distinction may help opener assess slam prospects.

Partnership Bidding

How should the following hands be bid, using the methods on page 78 and using Roman Key Card Blackwood methods (*see* pages 76–77)? West is the dealer on each hand and neither side is vulnerable.

WEST	EAST	WEST	EAST
1. ♠ 7 ♡ 63 ◇ 975 ♣ KQJ8642	1. ♠ AKQ6 ♡ AK75 ◇ KQ ♣ 953	7. ♠ KQ109652 ♡ 7 ◇ 84 ♣ J102	7. ♠ 4 ♡ AKQJ862 ◇ KQ ♣ AKQ
2. ♠ 7 ♡ 63 ◇ 975 ♣ AKJ8642	2. ♠ AKQ6 ♡ AK75 ◇ KQ ♣ 953	8. ♠ KQJ97642 ♡ 8 ◇ 64 ♣ A3	8. ♠ 3 ♡ AKQ95 ◇ A752 ♣ KQ2
3. ♠ QJ109543 ♡ 5 ◇ Q86 ♣ 62	3. ♠ 872 ♡ AKQJ ◇ 4 ♣ AKJ75	9. ♠ 7 ♡ 64 ◇ 62 ♣ AKQJ7542	9. ♠ AKJ8 ♡ AK52 ◇ K873 ♣ 3
4. ♠ KQ109543 ♡ 5 ◇ Q86 ♣ 62	4. ♠ 872 ♡ AKQJ ◇ 4 ♣ AKJ75	10. ♠ 65 ♡ 7 ◇ 9 ♣ KJ10986432	10. ♠ AKJ8 ♡ AK52 ◇ K873 ♣ 5
5. ♠ AK96543 ♡ 7 ◇ J86 ♣ 64	5. ♠ 872 ♡ AKQJ ◇ 4 ♣ AKJ72	11. ♠ Q6 ♡ 932 ◇ AQ108642 ♣ 9	11. ♠ AKJ854 ♡ A8 ◇ — ♣ AKQJ3
6. ♠ AQ107652 ♡ 7 ◇ 1032 ♣ 86	6. ♠ 4 ♡ AKQJ862 ◇ KQ ♣ AKQ	12. ♠ 6 ♡ AKQ87642 ◇ 74 ♣ 32	12. ♠ A95 ♡ 53 ◇ AK86 ♣ AK54

Chapter 15

Defensive Bidding

Defensive bidding is not related to the system you play. Whether you play Acol or Precision or Five-Card Majors does not determine whether you play Weak Jump Overcalls, Intermediate Jump Overcalls, Unusual 2NT or whatever. You may choose any defensive bidding structure to go with your constructive bidding. The following are popular at duplicate.

Weak Jump Overcalls
   The jump overcall to the two-level or the three-level shows a good six-card or longer suit and about 6–10 HCP. The suit quality (Length + Honours) should equal the number of tricks being bid (suit quality 8 for the two-level, 9 for the 3-level).
   With a weak hand, partner will pass. Over a two-level jump, 2NT is used as Ogust (*see* page 43). At any level, change of suit is strong and forcing. A bid of the enemy suit is strong and asks for the overcaller to bid 3NT with a stopper in that suit.
   Hands worth an overcall outside the weak jump limits should simply overcall (about 8–15 HCP and a good suit – suit quality should equal the number of tricks bid) or double (double and change of suit over partner's reply shows 16 points up and a good five-card suit).
Double and bid again = 16 points or more and five losers.
Double and jump rebid = about 19 points or more and four losers.
   Jump raises of overcalls are generally played as pre-emptive rather than constructive. With a stronger hand, use the bid of the enemy suit. Thus:

WEST	NORTH	EAST	SOUTH	
1◇	1♠	Pass	3♠	The 3♠ bid is pre-emptive. Four trumps and eight losers is about the right holding.
1◇	1♠	Pass	2◇	With a strong raise in spades, start by bidding their suit. You can support on the next round.

The 1NT Overcall

This shows 16–18 HCP, a balanced hand and a stopper in their suit. A strong 15 HCP with a double stopper in their suit will do. Bidding after the 1NT overcall follows the same structure as after a 1NT opening.

Partnership Bidding

How should the following hands be bid, using the methods on page 80? There is no bidding by North–South other than that given. West is the dealer unless stated otherwise.

WEST	EAST	WEST	EAST
1. N opens 1♡	1. N opens 1♡	5. N opens 1♡	5. N opens 1♡
♠ 83	♠ AQJ76	♠ KJ742	♠ AQ963
♡ 8643	♡ K7	♡ 9643	♡ 72
◇ Q2	◇ AK43	◇ 72	◇ KQJ
♣ J9854	♣ 72	♣ A8	♣ J106
2. N opens 1◇	2. N opens 1◇	6. N opens 1♡	6. N opens 1♡
♠ Q852	♠ KJ10964	♠ K963	♠ AJ72
♡ A9832	♡ 7	♡ 84	♡ AQ3
◇ A95	◇ 642	◇ QJ1073	◇ K962
♣ 7	♣ A83	♣ Q7	♣ K8
3. N opens 1♣	3. N opens 1♣	7. N opens 1♣	7. N opens 1♣
♠ A765	♠ 82	♠ K8	♠ AJ973
♡ 86	♡ AQJ1074	♡ 764	♡ 853
◇ 9843	◇ KQJ	◇ 9732	◇ AJ104
♣ 642	♣ AK	♣ AJ107	♣ 2
4. Dealer S	4. Dealer S	8. Dealer S	8. Dealer S
S opens 1♡	S opens 1♡	S opens 1◇	S opens 1◇
♠ K97	♠ QJ5	♠ 95	♠ QJ72
♡ 7	♡ A1093	♡ AQJ93	♡ K1054
◇ 642	◇ AJ8	◇ 4	◇ AK9
♣ AQJ876	♣ K52	♣ K7653	♣ 42

Responsive Doubles

Where partner makes a takeout double and third player raises opener's suit, it is sensible to play double by fourth player as takeout. This second double for takeout is called a responsive double. If third player changes suit, double is for penalties. This is useful to expose a psychic response. The responsive double applies only if third player raises opener.

WEST	NORTH	EAST	SOUTH
1♡	Dble	2♡	Dble

South's double shows both minors. With spades, South would bid spades. After a major raise, a responsive double shows both minors. After a minor raise, a responsive double shows both majors.

The responsive double is best used up to the three level. Thus:

WEST	NORTH	EAST	SOUTH
1♢	Dble	3♢	Dble

Without a responsive double, South may have a tough decision which major to show. The responsive double allows South to show both.

Competitive Doubles

At duplicate it makes sense to use doubles of a suit bid at the one-level or two-level for takeout, almost regardless of the preceding auction. This makes competitive bidding much easier. The concept is simply an extension of negative doubles where responder's double of a suit bid at a low level is for takeout. The final double in each of these auctions is for takeout.

WEST	NORTH	EAST	SOUTH
1♢	1♡	2♣	Dble

South's double should have 5 spades and tolerance for hearts.

WEST	NORTH	EAST	SOUTH
1♢	Pass	1♡	2♣
Pass	Pass	Dble	

East figures to be short in clubs. East may have both majors but this is not the only pattern for the double.

WEST	NORTH	EAST	SOUTH
1♢	Pass	1♡	1♠
Dble			

West's double here implies three-card support for hearts. A bid of 2♡ would show four-card support. Any action other than 2♡ or double (e.g., 2♣ or 2♢) would deny even three-card support for hearts.

When you have a hand with which you would like to double their suit for penalties, you pass. When the bidding reverts to partner, you hope partner will be able to make a takeout double which you can then pass, converting it to penalties.

If playing this style, a double of a suit bid at the one-level or two-level is for penalties after a redouble or if an earlier double has been passed for penalties.

Partnership Bidding

How should the following hands be bid, using the methods on page 82? There is no bidding by North–South other than that given.

WEST	EAST	WEST	EAST
1. Dealer N N opens 1◇ S bids 2◇ ♠ AJ42 ♡ K643 ◇ 92 ♣ 863	1. Dealer N N opens 1◇ S bids 2◇ ♠ K763 ♡ Q72 ◇ J3 ♣ AKJ5	5. Dealer W N passes S bids 2◇ ♠ 6 ♡ AJ764 ◇ K3 ♣ KQ742	5. Dealer W N passes S bids 2◇ ♠ KQ873 ♡ 92 ◇ 54 ♣ A653
2. Dealer S S opens 1♡ N bids 2♡ ♠ AQ92 ♡ 2 ◇ KJ743 ♣ K72	2. Dealer S S opens 1♡ N bids 2♡ ♠ K7 ♡ 743 ◇ Q652 ♣ Q653	6. Dealer W N passes S bids 2◇ ♠ A86 ♡ Q942 ◇ 5 ♣ AK743	6. Dealer W N passes S bids 2◇ ♠ KJ742 ♡ 83 ◇ J762 ♣ J2
3. Dealer S S opens 1♡ N bids 2♡ ♠ K874 ♡ J3 ◇ KQ32 ♣ A96	3. Dealer S S opens 1♡ N bids 2♡ ♠ Q962 ♡ Q72 ◇ 86 ♣ K543	7. Dealer E S passes N bids 2♣ ♠ A932 ♡ K764 ◇ 742 ♣ 97	7. Dealer E S passes N bids 2♣ ♠ KQ54 ♡ J8 ◇ AJ98 ♣ K32
4. Dealer N N opens 1♡ S bids 3♡ ♠ 86 ♡ 4 ◇ KQ632 ♣ QJ653	4. Dealer N N opens 1♡ S bids 3♡ ♠ A732 ♡ 92 ◇ AJ5 ♣ K874	8. Dealer E S passes N bids 2◇ ♠ AJ982 ♡ 72 ◇ 4 ♣ Q7643	8. Dealer E S passes N bids 2◇ ♠ 6 ♡ KQ863 ◇ AJ762 ♣ K2

TWO-SUITED OVERCALLS

The Unusual 2NT

An immediate overcall of 2NT is used to show both minors, at least a 5–5 pattern. With a 5–5, the strength is about 8–12 HCP. With a 6–5, the strength might be weaker. Both suits should be respectable (about five honours between the two suits is a good guide). The bid is used to suggest a sacrifice in case the opponents bid game in a major. The hand should not contain more than two quick tricks. If it does, you have reasonable defence against their major.

The Delayed 2NT

Where the opponents have bid and raised a suit but the bidding has stopped at the two-level, you should usually compete and try to push them to the three-level. A delayed overcall shows at least a five-card suit (but the suit may be quite poor), a delayed double is for takeout, showing the missing suits and a delayed 2NT asks partner to choose a minor. A delayed 2NT may be only 4–4 in the minors (failure to bid 2NT earlier suggests the hand is not 5–5). The strength for any of these delayed actions is about 6 points or better. The fact that they have found a trump fit and stopped at the two level indicates each side has about half the points.

The Michaels Cue Bid

A bid of the enemy major suit shows a weak 5–5, with five cards in the other major and an undisclosed five-card minor. The strength is the same as for the unusual 2NT. With a weak hand, partner can bid the major shown or bid 3♣. With diamonds, the overcaller will revert to 3♦. With a strong hand, partner can bid 2NT to check on the minor and the strength of the hand.

A bid of the enemy minor suit shows a 5–5 hand with both majors. The strength is as above.

Many partnerships prefer to use the Michaels Cue Bid only for the major suits. The sequences (1♣):2♣ or (1♦):2♦ are used to show genuine overcalls. Given the frequency of artificial minor suit openings, this is a sensible approach.

The occasional powerhouse hand which used to be shown by bidding the enemy suit is now shown by doubling first, and bidding the enemy suit on the next round after partner's reply to the double. Any further action by the doubler is forcing.

Partnership bidding

How should the following hands be bid, using the methods on page 84? There is no bidding by North–South other than that given. Neither side is vulnerable.

WEST	EAST	WEST	EAST

1. Dealer N
   N opens 1♣
   S bids 2♣
   ♠ J86
   ♡ KQ63
   ♢ Q2
   ♣ Q743

1. Dealer N
   N opens 1♣
   S bids 2♣
   ♠ 73
   ♡ J2
   ♢ A9863
   ♣ KJ95

5. Dealer S
   S opens 1♣
   N passes
   ♠ 6
   ♡ AJ864
   ♢ KQJ62
   ♣ 43

5. Dealer S
   S opens 1♣
   N passes
   ♠ Q9752
   ♡ 7
   ♢ A54
   ♣ J765

2. Dealer S
   S opens 1♡
   N bids 2♡
   ♠ QJ43
   ♡ 72
   ♢ AJ986
   ♣ 62

2. Dealer S
   S opens 1♡
   N bids 2♡
   ♠ 72
   ♡ A53
   ♢ K105
   ♣ KJ873

6. Dealer N
   N opens 1♡
   S passes
   ♠ A7
   ♡ 9864
   ♢ AK53
   ♣ Q74

6. Dealer N
   N opens 1♡
   S passes
   ♠ K8542
   ♡ 73
   ♢ 8
   ♣ AJ1082

3. Dealer N
   N opens 1♡
   S bids 3♡
   ♠ 98653
   ♡ Q104
   ♢ K976
   ♣ 2

3. Dealer N
   N opens 1♡
   S bids 3♡
   ♠ 7
   ♡ 6
   ♢ AJ1083
   ♣ QJ7653

7. Dealer N
   N opens 1♡
   S bids 3♡
   ♠ A9832
   ♡ J763
   ♢ 7
   ♣ KQ9

7. Dealer N
   N opens 1♡
   S bids 3♡
   ♠ Q10765
   ♡ 8
   ♢ KQ8652
   ♣ 6

4. Dealer S
   S opens 1♠
   N bids 2♠
   ♠ 8
   ♡ Q8632
   ♢ J1076
   ♣ AK8

4. Dealer S
   S opens 1♠
   N bids 2♠
   ♠ 9752
   ♡ 9
   ♢ AQ83
   ♣ QJ62

8. Dealer S
   S opens 1♡
   N passes
   ♠ AKJ82
   ♡ 7
   ♢ AJ
   ♣ AKQJ2

8. Dealer S
   S opens 1♡
   N passes
   ♠ —
   ♡ J105
   ♢ 95432
   ♣ 87543

Answers to Exercises and Bidding Practice

Page 17
1. No bid 2. 1◇ 3. 1♠ 4. 1♠ 5. 1♠ 6. 1♡ 7. 1♡ 8. 3♡ vulnerable, 4♡ not vulnerable 9. 4♠ at any vulnerability 10. 1♡. Three quick tricks (A-K plus an ace) is enough to open the bidding. 11. 1♡ 12. 1♠. With a minimum opening and poor suits it is better to open 1♠ and rebid 2♡, keeping the bidding lower than opening 1♡ and rebidding 2♠.

Page 19
A. 1. 1NT 2. 3♡ 3. 2♣. Too strong for a raise to 2♡, but do not give a jump raise with only three trumps. Bid 2♣ now and raise hearts on the next round. 4. 4♡. Excellent support, weak HCP and 7 losers. 5. 2♡ 6. 1♠. The spades are good, the heart support minimum.

B. 1. 2♠. Too weak for 2♡. 2. 2♣. Planning to jump to 4♠ on the next round. 3. 2♣. Planning to jump to 4♠ on the next round. With game values and support for the major, the sequence is change-suit-jump-to-game-in-the-major-next-round. There is no other way to show this strength hand. If you have no genuine suit to show, bid your cheapest three-card suit. 4. 3♣. With 16 HCP or more and support for opener's major, jump shift (jump-bid in a strong three-card suit if you have no real second suit) and support the major next round. 5. 2♣. A 2♡ response promises five hearts. Bid 2♣ and support opener's major on the next round. 6. 2♠. It is best to downgrade a 4–3–3–3 pattern by one point and treat this as spade support with 9 points only.

Page 21
A. 1. 2NT 2. 2♣. Strong enough for 2NT but you have no stopper in diamonds. 3. 2♣. Best to keep 2NT for 4–3–3–3 patterns. 4. 3NT. 4–3–3–3 and 13–15 points. 5. 2♣. Strength and shape right for 3NT but no stopper in diamonds. 6. 1♠. With four-card suits, choose the cheaper bid, not necessarily the lower-ranking suit.

B. 1. 1NT. Too weak for 2♣. 2. 2♣. Just enough and you plan to rebid 3♣. 3. 1NT. Too weak for a two-level bid. 4. 2♣. Cheapest suit with four-card suits. 5. 2♣. Not 2♡ with only four hearts. 6. 2◇. With 5–5, bid the higher suit first.

Page 23
A. 1. 2NT. Too strong for 1NT. 2. 4♠. Four-card support and only 4½ losers. (Count AQ doubleton as only half a loser.) 3. 2◇.

B. 1. No bid. Minimum points, poor shape (8 losers compared with the average of 7 losers for a minimum opening). 2. 4♡. 14 HCP warrants a game bid. 3. 4♡. Only 12 HCP but the singleton justifies game.

C. 1. No bid 2. 3NT. 3. 2♡. As the rebid is not forcing, it is preferable to show the major. If you bid 2◇, responder will not bid a 4-card heart suit, or even a 5-card heart suit.

D. 1. 2♠. After a 2-over-1 response, rebidding the major shows only a minimum opening; it does not promise an extra spade. The 2NT rebid would show 15–18 points. 2. 2♠. Too weak for 3♣ (beyond your 'barrier' of 2♠), which would show 16 points or more. 3. 2♡. As 2♡ is below your 2♠ barrier (*see* page 34), it does not promise more than a minimum opening.

Page 25
A. 1. No bid. After a one-level response, a change of suit by opener at the two-level below opener's barrier is not forcing. 2. 3♣. The raise to the three-level shows 10–12 points, not forcing. 3. 3NT. Balanced with the unbid suit well stopped. 4. 3◇. The jump in the fourth suit is game-forcing and shows at least 5–5 in the two suits. 5. 2♡. You could pass, but the 5-card major with honour-doubleton appeals more. 6. 2NT. Promises a stopper in the fourth suit.

B. 1. 2♡. You have shown your 10 points with 2♣, now you show the heart support. 2. 3♣ 3. 2♠. Fourth suit. You are too good for 3◇ and are worth 4◇. However, you should try for 3NT by using fourth-suit-forcing to ask for a spade stopper. 4. 2♠. Fourth suit. Enough for game but unsure of the best game. If partner bids no-trumps, choose 3NT rather than 4♡. 5. 2♠. Fourth suit. Too strong for 3♣ which is droppable. 6. 3NT.

Page 27
A. 1. 2♣. Do not bid 3NT when a major fit could exist. 2. 3♠. Shows the five-card major and forces to game. 3. 4♠. With six trumps and no slam prospects, insist on the major suit game. 4. 2♡. Sign-off. 5. 3NT. Do not introduce a minor suit with game values and no singleton. 6. 4NT. Invites 6NT if opener is not minimum. Opener

should pass with 15, bid 5NT with 16 and 6NT with 17.

B. 1. No Bid. **2.** 6NT **3.** 3NT. Do not introduce the minor. **4.** 3♣. Stayman. **5.** 4♡. **6.** 3◇. Forcing. You have slam prospects if partner can support diamonds.

Page 29

1. 1◇. With 4–4 minors, open 1◇. **2.** 1◇. No five-card major: open longer minor. **3.** 1◇. 4–4 minors. **4.** 1♣. With 3–3 minors, choose 1♣. **5.** 1♣. Even if the clubs are terrible. **6.** 1◇. Longer minor. **7.** 1NT. **8.** 1◇. **9.** 1◇. **10.** 1◇. **11.** 1♣. Longer minor. **12.** 1◇.

Page 31

A. 1. 1♡. There is no suit quality requirement. **2.** 1♠. Choose a major rather than 1NT. **3.** 1♠. Bid a major ahead of supporting a minor. **4.** 1◇. Longer suit comes first. **5.** 1◇. With four-card suits, bid the cheaper first. Over 1♡, you can raise; over 1♠, you rebid 1NT and over 1NT or 2♣ you will pass. If opener has hearts, this enables opener to play the hand. **6.** 1♡. With a 5–5 pattern, bid the higher suit first.

B. 1. 1♡. Bid a major before raising a minor. **2.** 1♡. Even if the minor support is excellent, the major is shown first. **3.** 1♠. Too weak for the natural 2♣. **4.** 2◇. Not quite enough for 3◇. **5.** 1♠. Any four-card major is biddable. **6.** 2◇. Support a minor rather than respond 1NT.

Page 33

A. 1. 2NT. 4–3–3–3, 11–12 points, no major. **2.** 1♠. Show the major rather than bid no-trumps. **3.** 3♣. 10–12 and 5+ clubs, no major. **4.** 3NT. **5.** 1◇. Enough for 3NT but no cover in spades. Over 1♠, you can bid 3NT. Over 1♡, use 2♠, fourth-suit-forcing. **6.** 1◇. You are too strong for 3♣ and 3NT is unattractive with no stopper in hearts. With this problem, change suit (choose a minor when bidding a fake suit, not a major).

B. 1. 1♡. Majors first. **2.** 2♠. The jump shift in a major shows at least a five-card suit and 16+ HCP. **3.** 1♠. **4.** 2♣. Too strong for 3◇ (*see* A/6). **5.** 3◇. **6.** 2♣. With a good hand, 10 points up, bid the suits in normal order, longer suit first.

Page 35

A. 1. 1♡. Four-card suits up-the-line. 2. 1♠. Bid a major rather than 1NT. 3. 1NT. Choose 1NT rather than 2♣ with a 5–3–3–2 pattern. 4. 3♢. Support partner rather than repeat your own suit. 5. 3♣. Too strong for just 2♣. Insufficient support to raise the diamonds. 6. 2NT. Shows 18–20 HCP, balanced, and is forcing to game.

B. 1. 1NT (*see* A/3). 2. 2♡. Shows 4 hearts, 5+ diamonds and 16+ points, forcing. 3. 2♢. Too weak for 2♡ which is beyond your barrier. 4. 2♣ 5. 3♣ 6. 4♠.

Page 37

1.
W	E
1♣	1♡
1♠	2♣
No	

West should rebid 1♠, not 1NT. 1NT would deny four spades. East gives preference back to clubs. The 2♣ bid shows 6–9 points and four or more clubs. With no prospects for game opposite 6–9 points, West passes.

2.
W	E
1♣	1♡
1♠	3♠
No	

East responds 1♡, up-the-line, with 4-card suits. West should not rebid 1NT. East's jump to 3♠ shows 4-card support and 10–12 points, the same sort of hand that would raise a 1♠ opening to 3♠. As West has a minimum, balanced opening, West passes 3♠.

3.
W	E
1♣	1♡
3♣	3NT
No	

East responds 1♡, up-the-line. West's 3♣ shows a 6-card suit and about 15–17 HCP. 13–14 HCP and a strong 7-card suit would also be enough. East has enough for game and with a balanced hand and stoppers in each suit outside clubs, chooses 3NT.

4.
W	E
1♢	1♡
2♣	2NT
3NT	No

West should rebid 2♣, not 1NT (unattractive with a 5–4–2–2 pattern unless most of your strength is in the short suits) and definitely not 2♢. 2NT by East, not forcing, shows 10–12 points including a stopper in the unbid suit. West has more than a minimum opening and enough to accept the invitation.

5.   w   E   East's 3♡ promises a 6-card suit and 10–12
     1◇   1♡   points. It is not forcing, but with doubleton
     1♠   3♡   support and sound values (A-K and A) in
     4♡   No   spades and diamonds, West should push on to
                   game. Even with clubs stopped West should
choose 4♡ with doubleton support.

6.   w   E   West should rebid 1♠, not 1NT. Show a
     1♣   1♡   4-card major rather than rebid 1NT. West's
     1♠   1NT   1♠ is not forcing but East should respond on
     No   almost all hands. With 4-card support, raise
the spades; without 4-card support, it is not attractive to leave
partner in spades.

    Treat the 1♠ rebid as though it were a 1♠ opening and reply
accordingly. You were strong enough to respond to 1♣ and so you
are strong enough to respond to 1♠. Pass only if your initial
response was below six points and you hold at least three spades.

7.   w   E   West's 2♡ showed at least 16 points including
     1◇   1♠   four hearts and 5+ diamonds. 2♡ is forcing for
     2♡   3◇   one round. East should choose 3◇, the known
     No   trump fit, rather than rebidding the spades
                   with 2♠. 3◇ is a weak rebid, indicating
6–8 points.

8.   w   E   East bids 1♡, up-the-line. West's 2◇,
     1♣   1♡   breathing the barrier (of 2♣), is a reverse,
     2◇   3NT   showing 16 points or more with at least five
     No   clubs and four diamonds. With both majors
                   stopped and enough for game, East bids 3NT.
2NT by East would be only 6–8 points.

9.   w   E   East has enough for game and bids 1♡ to try
     1◇   1♡   first for a major suit game. Over 2♣, East
     2♣   2♠   cannot bid no-trumps with nothing in spades
     2NT 3NT and so uses 2♠, fourth-suit-forcing, to obtain
     No   more information. West's 2NT shows a spade
stopper and only a minimum opening, but that is enough for East to
bid 3NT.

10. | w | E |
     |---|---|
     | 1♣ | 1♡ |
     | 1♠ | 2♢ |
     | 3♡ | 4♡ |
     | No | |

East has enough for game, but with five hearts and only one diamond stopper, East explores the best game via fourth-suit-forcing. West's 3♡ shows three hearts and better than a minimum opening.

11. | w | E |
     |---|---|
     | 1♣ | 1♡ |
     | 1♠ | 2♢ |
     | 3♣ | No |

With a hand similar to 10, East tries 2♢, fourth-suit-forcing. West's 3♣ shows a minimum opening hand with no stopper in diamonds and no secondary support for hearts. East has no reason to bid on.

12. | w | E |
     |---|---|
     | 1♣ | 1♡ |
     | 1♠ | 2♢ |
     | 2NT | No |

Again a similar East hand leads to 2♢, fourth-suit-forcing. West's 2NT shows a stopper in diamonds, but only a minimum opening hand. East has insufficient strength to go higher.

Page 39

1. | w | E |
    |---|---|
    | 2♣ | 2♠ |
    | 3♣ | 3♠ |
    | 4♠ | No |

With nine playing tricks, West has enough to open 2♣ and East has enough for a positive reply. West bids the clubs and East's 3♠ rebid indicates six spades. West supports and East does not have slam ambitions. With rare exceptions, the 2♣ opener leaves slam bidding to responder, as the 2♣ opening limited opener's hand in terms of trick potential.

2. | w | E |
    |---|---|
    | No | 2♣ |
    | 2♢ | 3♠ |
    | No | |

East has nine playing tricks in spades, West's 2♢ is a negative. East's 3♠ shows at least six spades, a strong suit, and exactly nine playing tricks. With no trick potential, West passes.

3. | w | E |
    |---|---|
    | No | 2♣ |
    | 2♢ | 3♡ |
    | 4♡ | No |

East has nine playing tricks in hearts, shown by the 3♡ rebid after West's 2♢ negative. West has a trick with the ace of diamonds and so raises East to game.

4. | w | E |
    |---|---|
    | 2♣ | 2♢ |
    | 3♡ | 4♡ |
    | No | |

West's 3♡ shows nine playing tricks with strong hearts. East has no high card trick, but has the potential to win one or more tricks by ruffing in spades. West is likely to take eleven tricks.

5. | W | E |
    |---|---|
    | 2♣ | 2♦ |
    | 3♡ | No |

West has the same hand as in 4 and uses the same 2♣:2♦, 3♡ route to show the nine playing tricks. East has no trick-taking potential and so passes.

6. | W | E |
    |---|---|
    | 2♣ | 2♦ |
    | 3NT | No |

West has nine playing tricks but as the tricks are INSTANT winners, West rebids 3NT. This rebid shows a long minor headed by A-K-Q and the potential to take nine tricks upon winning the lead. A rebid of 2NT would show the same hand type but only eight winners. The weak hearts could see 3NT fail, but it is unlikely and it is a good risk to take. 3NT figures to make on a spade lead or a diamond lead. Even on a heart lead the opponents may be unable to take five heart tricks.

With a singleton (other than the ace) or a void suit, the 3NT rebid is too risky. However, the risk is acceptable if you hold one rag doubleton suit.

7. | W | E |
    |---|---|
    | No | 2♣ |
    | 2♦ | 2NT |
    | 3NT | No |

East's 2NT rebid shows a solid minor and eight tricks on top. West has a potential winner with the ♣K and so raises to 3NT. The game is not sure but will succeed most of the time.

8. | W | E |
    |---|---|
    | No | 2♣ |
    | 2♦ | 4♡ |
    | No | |

East has nine tricks plus potential for a tenth via the ♦Q. If East opens 2♦, a negative response of 2♡ will make West declarer. It may pay to protect the diamond tenace, so East elects to open 2♣. East intends to look for slam opposite a positive response, but settles for game after a negative. It would be too timid for East to rebid only 3♡. When one useful jack will give game, bid the game. Notice West would in fact pass a 3♡ rebid.

9. | W | E |
    |---|---|
    | 2♣ | 3♣ |
    | 3♡ | 4NT |
    | 5♡ | 6♡ |
    | No | |

East's 3♣ is a positive, showing a 5+ suit and 8+ points (or 1½ quick tricks at least). Over 3♡, East sees slam potential and checks on aces before bidding the slam. At duplicate it would pay to continue with 5NT over 5♡ and finish in 6NT when West produces two kings.

10.

W	E
2♣	3♣
3♠	4NT
5♠	5NT
6◇	6♠
No	

East's 3♣ is a positive and East sees the slam potential when the spade fit comes to light. On learning that all the aces are held, East bids 5NT to try for a grand slam but settles for 6♠ when two kings are missing. Roman Key Card Blackwood (*see* Chapter 13, p.76) works much better in these cases.

11.

W	E
No	2♣
2◇	3◇
No	

East's 3◇ rebid shows at least six diamonds and about an 8½ to 9 playing-trick hand. West could be arrested for vagrancy (having no visible means of support) and so passes 3◇.

12.

W	E
2♣	2◇
4♣	5♣
No	

West's 4♣ rebid shows a powerful club suit and ten playing tricks. With the ♡K as potential for one trick, East raises to 5♣. Note that the ♡K might not be a sure winner. If East had the ♠K, East would still bid 5♣ but the ♠K might not be worth a trick. Bid on potential, not on certainty.

Page 41

1.

W	E
No	2◇
2♡	2♠
2NT	3♡
4♡	No

2◇ is artificial, 23 points or more. 2♡ is artificial, negative, less than 1½ quick tricks. 2♠ is natural and commits the partnership to game. 2NT denies spade support also denies a 5-card suit elsewhere. It would awful to pass 2♠. 3♡ = second suit. 4♡ = support.

2.

W	E
2◇	3♣
3♠	4♠
4NT	5♡
7NT	No

3♣ is a positive, 5+ clubs, 8+ points. 3♠ = 5+ spades. 4♠ = support. It is better for the stronger hand to ask 4NT. After a positive response to 2◇, the auction is slam-going if a trump fit is found. 4♠ is not droppable here.

3.

W	E
No	2◇
2♡	2♠
3♠	4♣
4♠	5◇
5♡	6♠
No	

West's 3♠ shows spade support plus some useful feature: an ace, a king, a singleton or a void. A jump to 4♠ would show support but no such useful feature. 4♣ is a cue bid showing the ♣A. 4♠ denies any ace outside trumps and denies the ♣K. 5◇ shows the ◇A and now 5♡ shows the ♡K or a singleton in hearts. That is enough for East.

4. | W | E |
|---|---|
| No | 2◇ |
| 2♡ | 2♠ |
| 4♠ | No |

West's 4♠ shows spade support but no ace, no king, no singleton, no void. That stops East venturing to the risky five-level. On 3, East could afford to go to the five-level as West's 3♠ had promised something useful.

5. | W | E |
|---|---|
| 2◇ | 3♣ |
| 3♡ | 3NT |
| 6NT | No |

East's 3♣ is a positive, 5+ clubs, 8+ points. 3♡ showed 5+ hearts. 3NT denies support, denies four spades or six good clubs and indicates minimum points (8–10). West has enough for 6NT.

6. | W | E |
|---|---|
| No | 2◇ |
| 2♡ | 2NT |
| 3NT | No |

East's 2NT rebid shows a balanced 23–24 points. 2NT is not forcing and further bidding is on the same lines as after a 2NT opening. West has a routine 3NT bid. 3NT might fail but is a reasonable contract. It makes if diamonds behave and either hearts are not led or the hearts break 4–3.

7. | W | E |
|---|---|
| 2◇ | 2♡ |
| 2♠ | 3♡ |
| 4♡ | No |

West's 2♠ rebid creates a game force. East's 3♡ denies spade support and shows five or more hearts. With three losers, 4♡ by West is enough. The 2◇ opening implied that strength and East can bid further if there are slam prospects.

8. | W | E |
|---|---|
| No | 2◇ |
| 3♣ | 3♡ |
| 3♠ | 4♣ |
| 4♠ | 4NT |
| 5◇ | 6♣ |
| No | |

3♣ is a positive with at least a 5-card suit. 3♠ denies heart support and 4♣ agrees clubs as trumps. 4♠ is a cue bid, showing the ♠A. 4NT asks for aces. Playing duplicate, East should continue with 5NT over 5◇ and bid 6NT over one or two kings. The risk is worth taking at pairs even opposite one king.

9. | W | E |
|---|---|
| 2◇ | 3♣ |
| 3NT | 4NT |
| 5♣ | 5NT |
| 6♡ | 7NT |
| No | |

3♣ is a positive. 3NT shows a balanced hand and no more than 23–24 points. This leaves it to responder to assess slam prospects. East checks on aces and kings and can count thirteen tricks via 6 clubs, 3 diamonds, 2 hearts and 2 spades.

10.

W	E
2◇	2♡
2♠	3♡
4NT	5◇
7♡	No

East's 2♡ is a negative, artificial. 3♡ shows a real suit, 5+ hearts, and denies support for spades. On hearing the heart suit, West asks for aces and can bid seven once East has the missing ace. If the ace is not with East, West would bid 6♡.

11.

W	E
No	2◇
2♡	2NT
3♣	3♡
3NT	4♠
No	

East's 2NT rebid shows 23–24 points, balanced, and is not forcing. West's 3♣ is Stayman and East shows hearts first. West bids 3NT as the use of 3♣ promises a major and since 3NT denies heart support, West must hold four spades. This allows East, with spades also, to bid 4♠ and be declarer.

12.

W	E
No	2◇
2♡	2NT
3♣	3♡
4♡	No

East's 2NT rebid again shows 23–24 balanced. With both majors, 4–4, 5–4 or 5–5, Stayman 3♣ is the best way to start. When East shows hearts, West supports. Had East bid 3◇, no major, West would then bid 3♠, showing five spades.

Page 43

1.

W	E
2♡	2NT
3♠	4♡
No	

West's 2♡ is a weak two, 6–10 HCP and a good 6-card suit, at worst Q-10 high. With support and more than 3 winners, responder should try for game. 2NT asks for opener's range. 3♠ says 'Maximum points and 2 top honours in my suit.'

2.

W	E
2♠	4♠
No	

With ten trumps and a shortage, responder should always bid at least game, whether weak (sacrifice) or strong (to make). This puts maximum pressure on the opponents who cannot tell after 2♠:4♠ whether responder is weak or strong.

3.

W	E
2♠	4♠
No	

East should bid at least 4♠ as the opponents hold at least 25 HCP, at least eight hearts and at least eight diamonds. The spades will be 1–1 or 2–0 so that the opponents can make at least a game, perhaps a slam. This is a good opportunity to psyche. East could try 3♡ (natural, forcing), planning to revert to spades later, or 4♡ (to play) if not vulnerable against vulnerable, or 4NT (asking for aces), intending to sign off when West shows insufficient aces for a slam!

4. | W | E |
   |---|---|
   | 2♠ | 3NT |
   | No | |

Even with two spades, 3NT figures to be a better spot when you hold a balanced hand and a double stopper in each outside suit. Here if spades do not break, 4♠ will fail, but 3NT might still come home.

5. | W | E |
   |---|---|
   | 2♡ | 2NT |
   | 3♣ | 3♡ |
   | No | |

With a doubleton heart and more than three winners, East has enough to try for a game. 3♣ shows minimum points and only one top honour in hearts. East gives up and signs off in 3♡.

6. | W | E |
   |---|---|
   | 2♡ | 2NT |
   | 3◇ | 6♡ |
   | No | |

2NT enquired about opener's range. 3◇ showed minimum points but two top honours in hearts. With only one spade to lose, East can count on 6 heart tricks, 2 diamonds, 3 clubs and either a spade ruff or an extra trick from the clubs.

7. | W | E |
   |---|---|
   | 2♡ | No |

With a shortage in the weak two suit, it is best to pass if you have less than 16 HCP.

8. | W | E |
   |---|---|
   | 2♡ | 2NT |
   | 3♠ | 4♡ |
   | No | |

With 4+ tricks, East enquires via 2NT. 3♠ shows maximum points and two top honours in hearts. It would be reasonable for East to bid 4♡ at once over 2♡ as East has four top tricks plus potential for a fifth via a club ruff. Five tricks is enough to bid game opposite a weak two.

9. | W | E |
   |---|---|
   | 2♡ | 2NT |
   | 3◇ | 3NT |
   | No | |

With four expected winners, East tries for game via 2NT. 3◇ shows minimum points, but two top honours in hearts. East knows that West has AKxxxx in hearts and precious little else. That adds up to nine tricks only so 4♡ is out, but as the nine tricks are instant winners, 3NT should be on.

10. W   E   Again with four winners, East uses 2NT to
     2♠   2NT   look for game. 3NT shows A-K-Q-x-x-x in
     3NT 4♠   spades and therefore little else. East has four
     No   winners to go with West's six, but 3NT would
                  be an error. As the lead has to be lost to set up
the club tricks, 3NT could fail on a red suit lead, while 4♠ should be
easy.

11. W   E   2NT = enquiry. 3♠ = maximum points and
     2♠   2NT   two top honours. 4♣ = cue bid, spades agreed
     3♠   4♣   as trumps. With a real club suit, bid 3♣ at once
     4♡   7NT   over 2♠. 4♡ = cue bid, ♡A. East can count
     No   13 tricks and so bids 7NT. If West is the sort of
                  player who might open 2♠ with a void, so that
4♡ could be a void in hearts, East should check back for aces via
4NT over 4♡.

12. W   E   With 7–10 points and 3-card support for
     2♠   3♠   opener, it may pay to pre-empt further by
     No   raising opener to the three-level. This is not an
                  invitation to game and opener must pass. It is
designed simply to make it tougher for the opponents to find their
best spot.

If interference has eliminated 2NT, then support at the three-level
is an invitation to game, e.g., 2♠ : (3◇) : 3♠ . . .

Page 45
A. 1.6. 2.6. 3.6. 4.8. 5.5. 6.5. 7.6. 8.7. 9.5.

B. i. 1. 3♠. 2. 4♡. You have seven playing tricks and, not
vulnerable, can gamble three more. 3. 1♡. Do not pre-empt when
you have enough high-card points for a one-opening. 4. 4♠. You
have eight playing tricks and can gamble three more when not
vulnerable, but do not pre-empt higher than game. 5. 1♠. Do not
pre-empt with four cards in the other major. 6. 4♠. A reasonable
gamble. ii. 1. 2♠. Six playing tricks is not enough for a three-level
pre-empt when vulnerable. You should have seven tricks. However,
a weak 2♠ is acceptable. 2. 3♡. 3. 1♡. 4. 4♠. 5. 1♠ or pass. 1♠ is
quite acceptable despite the low point count because of the excep-
tional shape. 6. 4♠. The expectancy is eight playing tricks and you
may gamble two more when vulnerable:
C. 1. 3NT 2. 3H 3. 5C. Further pre-empt and sacrifice.

Page 47

1.	W	E	2.	W	E	3.	W	E	4.	W	E
	3♠	No		3♠	5NT		3♥	4♥		5♦	No
				6♦*	7NT		No				
				*Two top honours							

5.	W	E	6.	W	E	7.	W	E	8.	W	E
	3♣	3NT		3♠	4♠		No	3NT		3NT	No
	No			No			4♣	4♦			
							No				

9.	W	E	10.	W	E	11.	W	E	12.	W	E
	3NT	5♣		3NT	5♣		3NT	6♦		3NT	7NT
	No			No			No			No	

Page 51

A. 1. 3♥. 2. 2♦. Avoid using 2NT with only three trumps. 3. 3♠. A splinter raise showing 4-card or better support, enough HCP for game and a singleton or void in spades. 4. 2NT. 10+ HCP plus support. 5. 2NT. There is no upper limit to the 2NT raise. 6. 3♥. The pre-emptive raise shows 6–9 HCP and at least four trumps.

B. 1. 4♠. Better than minimum opening but no slam ambitions. Responder can still bid on for a slam. 2. 3♣. A trial bid. You have enough for game but need help in clubs for a slam. If responder signs off in 3♠, slam is not likely. 3. 3NT. Blackwood, asking for aces. It does not make sense to use 3NT in its natural sense over the 2NT reply. 4. 3♠. Sign off with minimum points and no short suit. 5. 3♦. Trial bid, looking for help in diamonds. You intend to pass a 3♠ sign-off. 6. 3♣. Trial bid. Slam is highly likely if responder does not sign off in 3♠.

Page 53

1.	W	E
	1♠	2♣
	2♦	2NT
	No	

East's 2NT shows a stopper in hearts and about 10–12 points. With a minimum, West passes.

2. | W | E |
    |---|---|
    | 1♡ | 3NT |
    | 4♡ | No |

    3NT shows 15–17 points and a 3–3–3–4 or 3–3–4–3 pattern. West might pass 3NT but with a worthless doubleton, 4♡ will usually be safer. If the doubleton were Q-x or better, pass 3NT.

3. | W | E |
    |---|---|
    | 1♡ | 2♣ |
    | 2♢ | 3NT |
    | No | |

    With spades well held and no further interest in West's hand pattern, East jumps straight to 3NT over 2♢. With only one spade stopper, East should explore further using 2♠, fourth-suit-forcing.

4. | W | E |
    |---|---|
    | 1♠ | 2♢ |
    | 2♠ | 3NT |
    | No | |

    East bids the diamonds first, up-the-line with 4-card suits. West's 2♠ rebid does not promise an extra spade after a two-level response; it just shows a minimum opening and is not forcing. East has no reason to explore further and bids 3NT.

5. | W | E |
    |---|---|
    | 1♠ | 2♣ |
    | 2♢ | 2♡ |
    | 3♡ | 4♡ |
    | No | |

    Over 1NT, West might rebid 2♡ but, after a two-level response, it is better to bid up-the-line with 4-card suits as your rebid is forcing. 2♡ is fourth-suit-forcing and 3♡ confirms the 5–4–4–0 pattern. Without hearts, East would bid 3NT.

6. | W | E |
    |---|---|
    | 1♡ | 2♣ |
    | 2♢ | 2♠ |
    | 2NT | 3NT |
    | No | |

    East has a very strong hand but needs to know whether opener is minimum or stronger. Over 2♢, 2♠, fourth-suit-forcing, receives a 2NT reply, showing a spade stopper but minimum opening points. That dampens East's slam ambitions.

7. | W | E |
    |---|---|
    | 1♡ | 2♣ |
    | 2♢ | 2♠ |
    | 3NT | 6NT |
    | No | |

    East has the same hand as in 6. This time over 2♠, West jumps to 3NT, showing a spade stopper and better than a minimum opening. That is enough for East to bid the slam.

8. W   E   West's 2NT after passing still shows at least 10
    No   1♠   HCP and 4+ trumps. East's 3♠ is a sign-off,
    2NT   3♠   which West must observe. West could use 2♣
    No   Drury and East would bid 2◇ and pass West's
              2♠ rebid.

9. W   E   West's 3♣ shows a maximum pass, a strong
    No   1♡   5-card or longer club suit and support for
    3♣   4♡   opener's major. Although minimum in HCP,
    No   the good fit in clubs entitles East to bid the
              game.

10. W   E   After passing, 2♣ = 'Do you have a proper
    No   1♠   opening bid?' 2◇ = 'No, I don't', and so West
    2♣   2◇   signs off in 2♠.
    2♠   No

11. W   E   After 2♣ Drury, showing a maximum pass,
    No   1♠   2♡ = 4+ hearts and a sound opening, West
    2♣   2♡   shows spade preference and East bids the
    2♠   4♠   game.
    No

12. W   E   A new suit at the two-level after passing (other
    No   1♠   than 2♣ Drury) shows at least a five-card suit
    2◇   No   and denies support for opener's major.

Page 55

1. W   E   East's 2◇ is a transfer to hearts. Opener must
    1NT   2◇   accept the transfer even if the hearts were
    2♡   No   worthless. This is how responder signs off over
              1NT.

2. W   E   West's 2♡ is a transfer. The hand is likely to be
    No   1NT   better in spades than no-trumps. Even with a
    2♡   2♠   maximum, opener should do no more than
    No   accept the transfer with 2♠ when the pattern is
              4–3–3–3.

3.   W   E   With both majors 5–4/4–5/5–5 and a weak
     No   1NT   hand, it is better to use Stayman than to trans-
     2♣   2♡   fer. Here if East denies a major, West plans to
     No   sign off in 2♠. Your partnership needs to
                   agree that this is a sign-off sequence and not
                   encouraging.

4.   W   E   The transfer to diamonds is via 2NT. West bids
     1NT 2NT   3◇ with nothing special in diamonds or 3♣
     3◇   No   with a top honour in diamonds and maximum
                   points. With a genuine 2NT raise, East would
use 2♣ and rebid 2NT. Using transfers, 2♣ Stayman does not
promise a major suit and thus would need to be alerted.

5.   W   E   West's hand is too poor for a 3♣ opening but it
     No   1NT   must be safer to play in clubs than to leave it in
     2♠   3♣   1NT. The 2♠ response is the transfer to clubs.
     No   Opener bids 3♣ on most hands, but bids 2NT
                   with a top honour in clubs and a maximum
1NT. Here, East has the club honour but only minimum points,
hence 3♣.

6.   W   E   West's 2NT is the transfer to diamonds. East's
     No   1NT   3♣ shows a top honour in diamonds and a
     2NT 3♣   maximum 1NT. This enables West to try 3NT
     3NT No   with six running diamonds. 3NT is laydown,
but note how poor 3NT would be if East's diamonds were x-x.

7.   W   E   East's transfer followed by 2NT shows an invi-
     1NT 2◇   tational hand, 8–9 points, plus five hearts.
     2♡   2NT   With heart support, 16 points plus a double-
     4♡   No   ton, West has enough for game and chooses
                   hearts, not no-trumps.

8.   W   E   After a major suit transfer, opener may super-
     1NT 2♡   accept with a jump shift. This is used when
     3♠   4♠   opener has good support, maximum points
     No   and an outside doubleton (ruffing potential).

9. | W | E |
    |---|---|
    | No | 1NT |
    | 2♡ | 2♠ |
    | 3NT | 4♠ |
    | No | |

After the transfer, West's 3NT shows enough points for game plus five spades. Opener is asked to choose the better game. With 3-card support and a doubleton outside (ruffing potential), choose the major suit game.

10. | W | E |
    |---|---|
    | 1NT | 2♡ |
    | 2♠ | 3♢ |
    | 4♠ | No |

After the transfer, East's new suit is genuine and game-forcing. Opener's jump to game shows spade support but is weak in terms of slam potential. With two strong features (good trumps, maximum points, outside doubleton), opener would give strong preference (3♠), showing a hand more suitable for slam.

11. | W | E |
    |---|---|
    | 1NT | 2♡ |
    | 2♠ | 3♡ |
    | 4♡ | No |

After the transfer, showing five spades, East's 3♡ shows 4+ hearts and is forcing to game. West's 4♡ shows heart support but is weak for slam purposes. With good support and a maximum, West makes a cue bid (4♣ or 4♢ here), showing the bid suit ace and support for hearts. 3♠ or 4♠ would show spade support.

12. | W | E |
    |---|---|
    | 1NT | 3NT |
    | No | |

With a game hand, but with no slam potential, do not transfer to a minor. Transfer to a minor followed by 3NT over a weak acceptance (e.g., 1NT:2♠, 3♣:3NT) suggests a mild slam interest. Transfer to a minor followed by a raise to the four-level (e.g., 1NT:2♠, 3♣:4♣) is slam-going, sets the minor as trumps and asks opener to start cue bidding.

Page 57

1. | W | E |
    |---|---|
    | 2NT | 3♣ |
    | 3♢ | 3♠ |
    | 4♣ | 4♠ |
    | No | |

With five spades and four hearts, it is not suitable to use a transfer sequence, for after 2NT:3♡, 3♠ responder would not be sure whether 4♡ is safe. Over 3♣, if opener shows a 4-card major, responder raises. Over 3♢, a major suit by responder = 5-card suit. 4♣ by West showed spade support and the ♣A in case responder had slam in mind.

2.
W	E
No	2NT
3♡	3♠
4♠	No

After 2NT, West has enough to bid 4♠ but the transfer sequence enables the stronger hand to become declarer, often an advantage as the opening lead goes into strength.

3.
W	E
2NT	3◇
3♡	3NT
4♡	No

East's transfer then 3NT shows enough for game and a 5-card heart suit. Opener is asked to choose the better game. With heart support and a suit with just a bare stopper (clubs), opener chooses the major game.

4.
W	E
2NT	3♡
3♠	No

The transfer structure allows responder to sign off in a major at the three-level when responder has a worthless hand with a 5-card or 6-card suit. With a longer suit or 3+ points and 5+ suit, responder bids for game.

5.
W	E
No	2NT
3◇	4♡
No	

Where opener has game chances opposite no more than six rags, opener jumps to game in the major shown by the transfer. If opener bids 3♡ here, responder would pass, with an excellent game missed. Opener's strengths are 4-card support, ruffing potential with the doubleton club and instant winners, the aces and kings. Opposite six rags, East can count on six hearts, three outside aces plus an extra diamond trick.

6.
W	E
2NT	3♡
3♠	4◇
4♠	4NT
5♣	6♠
No	

East transfers to spades and bids 4◇ to show a genuine diamond suit. West shows preference for spades. East checks on aces and bids the slam when there are not two aces missing.

7.
W	E
2NT	3♠
4◇	4NT
5♠	6◇
No	

3♠ over 2NT shows slam interest with both minors. They need not be five-card suits and opener shows support only with 4-card support. Over 4◇, East checks on aces and bids 6◇ when there are not two aces missing.

8. W   E   East's 3♠ shows both minors and slam in-
    2NT   3♠   terest. 3NT denies support for either minor.
    3NT   4NT   4NT checks on aces and East bids 6NT. If
    5♠   6NT   responder had doubts about the best spot,
    No   responder could bid 4◇ over 3NT to check for
                  3-card support.

9. W   E   4◇ shows a one-suiter and slam interest. 4♡
    No   2NT   promises support for diamonds and the ♡A
    4◇   4♡   (cue bid). 5♣ = cue bid. 5◇ denies control in
    5♣   5◇   spades. 6◇ = 'I have spade control.'
    6◇   No

10. W   E   East has marginal slam ambitions but when
     2NT   4♣   West denies support for clubs with 4NT (not
     4NT   No   asking for aces), East gives up on slam.

11. W   E   West transfers to spades and with no slam aim
     No   2NT   intends to rebid 3NT. East's 4♠ shows great
     3♡   4♠   support, maximum points plus a ruffing poten-
     4NT   5♠   tial. West asks for aces and bids the slam. The
     6♠   No   super-accept jump to 4♠ is used not only to
                  ensure reaching game (*see* hand 5), but also to
help responder to look for slam on borderline hands.

12. W   E   With 5–5 in the majors and hopes beyond
     No   2NT   game, West should not use a transfer sequence
     3♣   3♡   (2NT:3♡, 3♠:4♡ could be passed by
     4NT   5♠   opener). On finding the fit, responder checks
     6♡   No   on aces and bids the slam. Had East bid 3◇
                  over 3♣, West would continue with 3♠, ask-
ing for 3-card support. With no spade fit, West would ask for aces
and then bid 6♡ if East had at least three aces.

Page 59

1. W   E   Playing 5-card major Stayman, West's 3♠ re-
   2NT   3♣   ply shows five spades and East naturally raises.
   3♠   4♠   Had West bid 3◇ (at least one 4-card major)
   No   East would bid 3♠ (to show hearts).

2. | W | E |
    |---|---|
    | 2NT | 3♣ |
    | 3♠ | 3NT |
    | No | |

West's 3♠ shows five spades. East does not have support and West will not hold four hearts as well as five spades, so East signs off in 3NT.

3. | W | E |
    |---|---|
    | No | 2NT |
    | 3♣ | 3♡ |
    | 4♡ | No |

East's 3♡ shows five hearts and naturally West supports. Had East bid 3◇, West would bid 4◇ showing both majors and asking opener to bid the major held or the better suit if opener also holds both majors.

4. | W | E |
    |---|---|
    | No | 2NT |
    | 3♣ | 3NT |
    | No | |

East's 3NT rebid shows no 5-card major and no 4-card major. If West is 5–3 in the majors, it is more practical to transfer to show the 5-card suit than to use 3♣. It is more likely that opener has 3-card support than a 5-card major.

5. | W | E |
    |---|---|
    | No | 2NT |
    | 3♣ | 3♠ |
    | 4♠ | No |

It is important that West uses 3♣ on hands like these. It is all too easy to bid 3NT and miss the superior 4♠ game.

6. | W | E |
    |---|---|
    | 2NT | 3◇ |
    | 3♡ | 3NT |
    | 4♡ | No |

With a 5-card major, use the transfer auction. With 3-card support for hearts and a doubleton, West should choose the major suit game.

7. | W | E |
    |---|---|
    | No | 2NT |
    | 3♣ | 3◇ |
    | 3♡ | 4♠ |
    | No | |

East's 3◇ denies a 5-card major, but shows at least one 4-card major. West bids 3♡, the major suit not wanted. This is to allow the stronger hand to become declarer if a 4–4 fit exists. With spades, East bids the game.

8. | W | E |
    |---|---|
    | 2NT | 3♣ |
    | 3◇ | 3♠ |
    | 3NT | No |

West's 3◇ = no 5-card major but at least one 4-card major. 3♠ = not interested in spades. 3NT indicates that spades is the suit held by opener.

9. | W | E |
    |---|---|
    | No | 2NT |
    | 3♣ | 3◇ |
    | 4◇ | 4♠ |
    | No | |

3◇ = no 5-card major, but at least one 4-card major. 4◇ = have 4–4 in the majors. East bids the major held.

10.
W	E
2NT	3♣
3♢	4♢
4♡	No

East's 4♢ again shows both majors. West chooses the stronger suit. With mirror hands (identical patterns), there is no chance to ruff or to set up length tricks.

11.
W	E
No	2NT
3♣	3♢
4♢	4♡
4NT	5♡
6♡	No

With 4 spades–5 hearts, use a transfer sequence, but with 5 spades–4 hearts, use the 3♣ structure. West shows both majors with 4♢ and bids on to slam after opener shows the hearts. Roman Key Card Blackwood would be useful here (Chapter 13, p.76).

12.
W	E
2NT	3♢
4♡	4NT
5♠	5NT
6♣	7♡
No	

With 4 spades–5 hearts, the transfer sequence is simpler. Over 3♢, West should give a super-accept jump to 4♡. Imagine partner has six rag hearts. If you have a good play for game opposite that, you are worth the jump accept.

Opposite six rags, West counts six hearts, ♠A, ♣A-K for 9 tricks, the tenth coming from a finesse in either minor or via a diamond ruff. After 6♣, East sees twelve top tricks, a ruff in West providing the thirteenth.

Page 61

A. 1. 3♣. Pre-emptive jump raise. 2. 3NT. Shows 15–17 points and a 3–3–3–4 or 3–3–4–3 pattern. Any further action is up to opener. 3. 1♠. Do not choose a 3NT reply when you hold a 4-card major. 4. 3♣. Pre-empt. 5. 2NT. Shows 10+ points and support for opener's minor. For clubs, there should be at least five clubs. 6. 2NT. Same as 5. Hand 5 will always move on to game, but Hand 6 will pass a 3♣ sign-off by opener.

B. 1. 2NT. For diamonds, 4-card support is enough. 2. 1♡. Do not bypass a 4-card major, no matter how weak. 3. 3NT. 15–17 points and 3–3–4–3 or 3–3–3–4. 4. 3♢. Pre-emptive raise, 6–9 points plus support. 5. 2NT. 10+ points and support for diamonds. Too strong for 3♢. 6. 2NT. You will bid on to at least game in no-trumps or diamonds. If partner attempts to sign off in 3♢, you will bid 3♡ next to show the heart stopper, aiming to reach 3NT if partner has the spades stopped.

Page 63

A. 1. No. No reason to bid again opposite 6–9 points. **2.** 3NT. Shows 18–20 balanced and all suits outside clubs stopped. **3.** 2♦. After suit agreement (2♣), a new suit is forcing. After minor suit agreement a new suit shows a stopper in it and is looking for 3NT. If partner can bid 2♥ to show a heart stopper, you play in 3NT. If partner bypasses the hearts, you should avoid 3NT. **4.** 2NT. An invitation to 3NT promising stoppers in all outside suits. Partner may pass or sign off in 3♣ or try 3NT with a maximum. **5.** 3NT. Given that partner should have the ♣K, you have eight top tricks and a heart lead or any extra king in partner's hand will give you nine. **6.** 2♥. Showing a stopper in hearts and simultaneously denying a diamond stopper. Stoppers are shown up-the-line.

B. 1. No. Not enough for game opposite only 6–9 points. **2.** 3♥. Shows a heart stopper and denies a diamond stopper in the quest for 3NT. **3.** 3NT.

C. 1. 3♦. Prepared to sign off opposite 10–11 points. **2.** 3NT. A reasonable gamble. **3.** 3♠. Shows spades stopped, denies stoppers in clubs/hearts.

Page 65

	W	E	
1.	1♦	1♥	East shows the major at once. Prefer a major
	1♠	2NT	suit bid to a no-trump bid. Likewise West
	No		rebids 1♠ and not 1NT. East's 2NT invites
			game but with a minimum, West declines.

	W	E	
2.	1♦	1♥	East has enough for a game but over 1♠, the
	1♠	2♣	correct game is not clear to East. 2♣ is fourth-
	2♥	4♥	suit-forcing. West's 2♥ shows 3-card support
	No		for hearts but only minimum opening points.
			East has enough for game.

	W	E	
3.	1♣	1♠	With a 5–3–3–2 West should rebid 1NT and
	1NT	2♣	not 2♣. East's 2♣ is an artificial game try and
	3♣	3NT	West's 3♣ shows five clubs and maximum
	No		points for the 1NT rebid. East has no aims
			other than 3NT.

4. | W | E |
    |---|---|
    | 1♣ | 1◇ |
    | 1NT | 2♣ |
    | 2◇ | No |

East's 2♣ is the artificial game try. 2◇ by West shows a minimum opening, 11–12 or a poor 13. As East has five diamonds, East takes the opportunity of passing. At pairs, East may prefer to chance 2NT.

5. | W | E |
    |---|---|
    | 1♣ | 1♠ |
    | 1NT | 2NT |
    | 3♡ | 4♡ |
    | No | |

As 2♣ takes care of the game invitational hands, 2NT is not needed as an invite to 3NT and is used as an artificial game force. West bids features up-the-line. 3♡ shows a 4-card heart suit. It also denies five clubs and four diamonds.

6. | W | E |
    |---|---|
    | 1♣ | 1♠ |
    | 1NT | 3♡ |
    | 4♡ | No |

East's jump to 3♡ is forcing to game and shows 5–5 in the majors. West could choose 4♠ or 4♡. As the hearts are fractionally better, choose the hearts.

7. | W | E |
    |---|---|
    | 1◇ | 1♡ |
    | 1NT | 2♣ |
    | 2◇ | 2♡ |
    | No | |

With 10 HCP and a 5-card suit. East has just enough to use the 2♣ rebid. West's 2◇ shows a minimum opening. East shows five hearts with 2♡ and West has no reason to push higher.

8. | W | E |
    |---|---|
    | 1◇ | 1♡ |
    | 1NT | 2♣ |
    | 2♡ | 3NT |
    | No | |

East's 2♣ shows 10–12 points. West's 2♡ shows a maximum 1NT rebid with three hearts. East prefers to play it in 3NT rather than in the 4–3 heart fit.

9. | W | E |
    |---|---|
    | 1♣ | 1♠ |
    | 1NT | 2♣ |
    | 2♠ | 4♠ |
    | No | |

East is too strong to rebid 2♡ over 1NT. That would show only 6–9 points. West's 2♠ shows 3-card support and a maximum 1NT. If West bid 2◇, minimum, East would bid 2♡ and West could then choose 2♡, 2♠ or 2NT.

10. | W | E |
    |---|---|
    | 1♣ | 1◇ |
    | 1♡ | 2♣ |
    | 2◇ | 2♡ |
    | No | |

East bids 1◇, 4-card suits up-the-line. This is more efficient than showing the major first. Over 1♡, East uses 2♣ to check opener's range. When opener shows a minimum, East signs off in 2♡.

11.

W	E
1◇	1♡
1♠	3♣
3NT	No

East's 3♣ shows enough points for game and at least 5–5 in hearts and clubs. With all the strength in the other two suits, West chooses 3NT. The more strength you hold opposite partner's known short suits, the more attractive it usually is to play in no-trumps.

12.

W	E
1◇	1♠
1NT	2NT
3♠	4♠
No	

East's 2NT is artificial, forcing to game. East uses this route to check whether West has 3-card spade support. When West reveals it, East bids game in spades. If West had rebid 3♣, 3◇ or 3♡, East would bid 3♠. A rebid of 3NT by West would show a 3–3–4–3 pattern with three rag spades and stoppers in each of the other suits.

Page 67

1.

W	N	E	S
1◇	Dbl	Rdbl	2♣
No	No	Dbl	No
No	No		

East's redouble aims for penalties. East's hand-type is ideal: short in partner's suit and strong in the other suits. West passes 2♣ to give partner a chance to double them. East's double is for penalties. After a redouble, all doubles are penalty doubles.

2.

W	N	E	S
1◇	1♠	2♠	No
2NT	No	3NT	No
No	No		

East's 2♠ shows at least the values for a 2NT bid but denies a stopper in spades. 2♠ also denies four hearts (as 2NT would). With four hearts, East would double 1♠. West's 2NT promises a stopper in spades but only minimum points. East has enough to bid the game.

If East had the same type of hand but with only three diamonds, say ♠ 872 ♡ A93 ◇ AJ7 ♣ KQ63, East would just change suit with 2♣. If necessary, East could bid spades later to ask for a spade stopper.

3.

W	N	E	S
1◇	1♠	2NT	No
3◇	No	No	No

East's 2NT has its usual meaning (10+ points and diamond support) but it also promises a spade stopper. West's 3◇ shows a minimum opening. As East is also minimum, East passes. It is possible that 3NT makes, but it is a poor contract. Even 3◇ is not a sure thing.

4.

W	N	E	S
1◇	1♡	2♡	No
5◇	No	No	No

East's 2♡ shows 10+ points with support for diamonds, but denies a stopper in hearts. With no stopper in hearts either, West gives up on 3NT and takes a shot at 5◇ which on the actual cards is an excellent contract. 3NT would fail if North has the 5+ hearts expected for the overcall. If West had a partial stopper such as J-x-x or Q-x, West could bid 3♡ over 2♡, asking East to bid 3NT if holding a half-stopper as well. Thus 3NT could be reached if East–West have a combined holding of J-x-x opposite Q-x, for example.

5.

W	N	E	S
1♣	1♠	Dbl	2♠
No	No	Dbl	No
3♡	No	4♡	No
No	No		

East's double is for takeout and shows four hearts. Over 2♠, West is too weak to bid at the three-level. East should contest the bidding, even on minimum strength if 2♠ is passed back to East. In fact, East has a strong hand but the best continuation is a further double. If East were a bit stronger, East would rebid 3♠, forcing to game and asking for a spade stopper for no-trumps (over which West would bid 4♡). In reply to the double, West bids 3♡ and it would be timid for East to pass with 12 HCP and a doubleton.

6.

W	N	E	S
1◇	1♠	Dbl	No
1NT	No	3NT	No
No	No		

East's double shows four hearts and is for takeout. West's 1NT is natural and shows a spade stopper. That is enough for East to bid 3NT.

If West had the same strength and shape but no spade stopper, West should find some rebid other than 1NT. If West's rebid were 2♣ or 2◇, East could then follow up with 2♠, a game-force asking for a spade stopper (as West's suit rebid may be based on an unbalanced hand unsuitable for a 1NT rebid).

7.

W	N	E	S
1◇	2♣	Dbl	No
No	No		

East's double is for takeout. 'Negative double' is an unfortunate choice of name. Preferable would be 'Responder's double' which is exactly what it is. East's double shows the majors. It is recommended you should have at least 4–4 in the majors when you double a minor over partner's suit opening. However, some partnerships do permit 4–3 holdings in the majors.

As West is short in the majors and loaded in clubs, West passes the double out for penalties. This is one of the benefits of using responder's double for takeout. Otherwise, if East were to bid 2♡, say, North escapes the axe.

8.

W	N	E	S
1◇	2♣	Dbl	No
3♣	No	3NT	No
No	No		

East's double is for takeout and shows the majors. West has enough for game but no major. 3♣ is forcing to game and asks for a club stopper. 3NT shows a club stopper.

Page 69

1.

W	E
No	2♣
2◇	2NT
3♣	3♠
4♠	No

East's 2♣ opening is forcing to game and the 2NT rebid shows 25 HCP and a balanced hand. It is still forcing. West's 2◇ is a negative and 3♣ over 2NT is Stayman, asking for a 4-card major. East shows the spades and West raises to 4♠.

Note the superiority of 4♠ over 3NT. With other methods, East–West might bid 2♣:2◇, 3NT which West would pass. 3NT might even fail on a heart lead and 4♠ will certainly score better at pairs.

2.

W	E
2♣	2◇
2NT	3♣
3♡	3NT
No	

2♣ = game force; 2◇ = negative. 2NT = balanced and 25+ points. 3♣ = Stayman and 3♡ shows four hearts. 3NT denies heart support, indicating four spades as Stayman was used. West passes 3NT, but if West had four hearts and four spades, West could bid 4♠.

East's sequence (rather than 3♠ over 3♡) allows the strong hand to be the declarer in 4♠.

3. | W | E |
    |---|---|
    | No | 2♣ |
    | 2♦ | 2NT |
    | 3♦ | 3♡ |
    | 3♠ | 4♡ |
    | No | |

2♣ = game force; 2♦ = negative. 2NT = balanced, 25+ points. It is still forcing. Further bidding proceeds as over a natural 2NT opening (*see* pages 56–58). 3♦ is a transfer to hearts and 3♠ shows four spades. East shows preference for hearts and as East is minimum, East leaves any slam decisions to West (no slam desires with such a weak hand).

4. | W | E |
    |---|---|
    | 2♣ | 2♦ |
    | 2NT | 4NT |
    | 6NT | No |

Over 2NT, showing 25+ points, East is too good to bid just 3NT. Bid 3NT with 0–3 points, 4NT with 4–5, 5NT with 6–7 and with 8+ give a positive response initially. West would pass 4NT if minimum. On the actual hand, West has enough to bid 6NT. With 28 points, West might bid 5NT asking East to bid on only with five points (or 4 HCP plus a 5-card suit). Missing an ace and a king, West knows 7NT will not be a good bet. With an ace plus a king, East would have a positive response.

5. | W | E |
    |---|---|
    | No | 2♣ |
    | 2♦ | 2NT |
    | 3♡ | 3♠ |
    | 4♠ | 4NT |
    | 5♣ | 6♠ |
    | No | |

Over 2NT (25+ points, balanced, forcing), West's 3♡ is a transfer to spades. East can afford to bid just 3♠ as auctions starting with 2♣ are forcing to game, no exceptions. West's 4♠ shows a poor hand with a 6-card suit. East can see slam potential opposite even a yarborough including six spades. East has seven `winners outside spades and if spades are 2–2 or North has ace singleton, there will be five spade tricks. If there are no nasty breaks, it may be possible to lead spades twice from West and thus score the slam even if North has A-x-x. Just in case West has the ♠A, East asks for aces. 5♣ shows no ace, so East settles for 6♠. Had West shown an ace, East would bid 7NT.

6. | W | E |
    |---|---|
    | 2♣ | 2♦ |
    | 2NT | 3♡ |
    | 3♠ | 4♣ |
    | 4♦ | 5♣ |
    | 6♣ | No |

East's 3♡ is a transfer to spades. Over 3♠, 4♣ shows a genuine club suit. West's 4♦ cue bid shows support for clubs and the ♦A. East's 5♣ is meant as a sign-off but West can chance the slam. East will either be 5–4 in the black suits with a few points or 5–5 in the black suits with very little. Even if East does not have the ♣Q, the slam hinges on a 2–2 club break.

7.

W	E
No	2♣
2NT	3◇
3♡	3♠
4♠	5♣
5◇	7◇
No	

2NT = positive, balanced, 8+ points. 3◇ = genuine suit. 3♡ = cue bid: diamond support plus the ♡A. 3♠ = cue bid, ♠A. 4♠ = cue bid showing the ♠K and denying any other ace and denying the ♡K. 5♣ = cue, ♣A. 5◇ = no other control to show. After ♡A and ♠K with West, East could bid 7◇ at once. East's 5♣ was angling for 7NT if West bid 6♣ showing the king of clubs. East could have just asked for aces and kings over 3♡. Likewise, if West bids 4◇ over 3◇, East would bid 4NT and 5NT and settle for 7◇ when West shows only one king.

8.

W	E
No	2♣
3◇	3♡
3NT	4NT
5◇	5NT
6◇	6NT
No	

West's 3◇ is a positive, 8+ points or 1½ quick tricks (as here) plus 5+ diamonds. 3♡ = 5+ hearts. 3NT denies support for hearts, shows no useful second suit and denies six diamonds. East checks on aces and kings and settles for 6NT. When the slam values are clearcut, choose 6NT and not 6-suit. Had West shown two kings, East would bid 7NT.

9.

W	E
2♣	3♡
4NT	5◇
7NT	No

3♡ shows a strong 6+ suit playable opposite a singleton. West checks to make sure East has the ♡A. With six heart winners together, West can count on four diamonds and two black aces. The thirteenth trick can come from the long diamond or the club finesse.

10.

W	E
2♣	3♠
4NT	5♣
6♠	No

3♠ shows a strong single-suiter. West checks on aces, settles for 6♠. Note that 6NT would be foolish here. As 3♠ shows a suit playable opposite a singleton, West's doubleton is adequate support.

11.

W	E
No	2♣
2◇	4♠
No	

With only three losers, East has enough to open 2♣. After the 2◇ negative, East knows slam cannot be a good bet as West cannot have as much as an ace and a king and East is missing two aces and a king.

12.

W	E
2♣	2♦
2♠	4♣
4NT	5♦
7♠	No

East's 4♣ is a splinter raise, showing support for spades and a singleton or a void in clubs. As East has given a 2♦ negative, it would not make sense now to have 4♣ as a genuine club suit. West checks on aces and on finding East has the ♡A, West can see-that there are no losers in spades, hearts or diamonds and the club losers can be ruffed in dummy.

Page 71

A. 1. 2♠. Too strong for a 1♠ opening, but not enough to insist on game. A good test on whether to open 2♣ is: 'If partner has a 4–3–3–3 yarborough, would I want to be in game?' Here West has three top losers opposite a yarborough and even if you could reach the dummy, how would you take two finesses?
2. 2♣. With 24 HCP you have too much to open 2♠.
3. 2♡. You intend to rebid 4♦ if possible. Although you have only 3 losers (2½ if you count the diamonds as only half a loser because of the supporting J-10), it would be short-sighted to open 2♣. As you have such a freak hand, it is highly likely you will encounter interference bidding in the black suits. Having opened 2♡, you can compete safely over 4♠ or 5♣ by bidding 5♦ on the next round. Imagine you opened 2♣ and the opponents then bid 3♣:5♣ with partner passing. How would you cope now?
4. 2♡. If partner bids 2NT, you plan to rebid 3♠ which is forcing.
5. 1♠. The hand is worth a jump shift to 3♡ next, but the spades are too weak for a 2♠ opening.
6. 2♠. Rebid 4♠ after a 2NT reply. The hand is too strong for a 4♠ opening and also too much to open 1♠.

B. 1. 2NT. The 2♡ opening is forcing. Opposite a hand like A/3 or A/4 you would hate to stop in 2♡. 2. 4♡. The jump to game in opener's major after 2♡ or 2♠ shows support and two kings, no aces. 3. 3♡. Slam is highly likely opposite a nine-trick hand.

C. 1. 3♦. A positive response showing at least five diamonds. Slam is likely if you find a fit with one of your suits. 2. 4♣. After a 2♡ or 2♠ opening, it makes sense to play jump-shift responses as splinters. 4♣ shows a positive response, support for spades and a singleton or void in clubs. 3. 2NT. Choose the negative response. You can support the spades on the next round.

Page 73

1.
W	E
2♦	2♥
No	

West's 2♦ is the multi. East's 2♥ says, 'If you have a weak two in hearts, this is as far as I want to go.' As West does have a weak 2♥, West passes.

2.
W	E
2♦	2NT
3NT	No

East's 2NT is a strong enquiry, normally a strong opening hand. With support for both majors, a hand with better than three tricks is enough. East has ruffing potential if West's suit is hearts. When West shows a suit headed by the A-K-Q (must be spades, of course), East is delighted to pass 3NT, which should be child's play.

3.
W	E
2♦	2♥
2♠	No

2♥ = Pass with a weak two in hearts. 2♠ = I have a weak two in spades. Pass = I am still not interested in bidding further.

4.
W	E
2♦	2♥
2NT	No

2♥ = Pass if you have the weak two in hearts. 2NT = No, I have 23–24 points and a balanced hand. With no points at all, East passes. Bidding after the 2NT rebid would follow the same structure as after a natural 2NT opening (*see* pages 56–58).

5.
W	E
No	2♦
2♥	2NT
3♣	3♠
4♠	No

2♥ = To play opposite a weak 2♥. 2NT = 23–24 points, balanced, not forcing. 3♣ = Stayman and 3♠ = four spades.

6.
W	E
No	2♦
2♥	3♣
3NT	No

2♥ = To play if East has a weak two in hearts. 3♣ = an Acol Two in clubs, 8–9 playing tricks if clubs are trumps. 3NT = a sensible shot opposite a nine-trick hand. On a spade lead or a heart lead, 3NT makes easily. On a diamond lead and a spade back, you could be several off, but the chances of that happening are small. 3NT by West is far better than 3NT by East.

7.
W	E
2♦	2NT
3♠	3NT
No	

2NT is a strong enquiry and 3♠ shows a weak two in spades with minimum points and only one top honour in spades. East has a comfortable 3NT rebid. 3NT figures to be at least as good as 4♠. The opening lead coming to East may be worth an extra trick.

8.
W	E
2♦	2♠
No	

2♠ = Pass if you have a weak two in spades. East expects West to have the weak 2♠, but if West happened to have a weak two in hearts, East would want to compete to a high level,

subject to vulnerability. As West has the weak 2♠, West passes. Over 2♠, West would bid 2NT with 23–24 balanced, 3♣/3♦ with the Acol Two hand, 3♡ with a minimum weak two in hearts and 4♡ with a maximum weak two in hearts.

9.
W	E
2♦	2NT
4NT	7NT
No	

2NT is a strong enquiry. 4NT = 23–24 balanced. This will be a rare occurrence for opener to have the huge balanced hand and hear the strong 2NT reply. With 14 HCP opposite 23–24, East has enough for 7NT.

10.
W	E
2♦	2♠
3♦	4♦
4♠	4NT
5♡	5NT
6♡	6NT
No	

East is not interested opposite a weak two in spades, but has some interest if West has a weak two in hearts. 2♠ = To play opposite a weak 2♠. 3♦ = Acol Two in diamonds. 4♦ is strong and shows support. 4♠ = cue bid, ♠A. 4NT/5NT = Blackwood for aces and kings.

11.
W	E
2♦	2NT
4♠	No

2NT = strong enquiry. 4♠ = strong suit (four honours usually), playable opposite a singleton.

12.
W	E
2♦	2NT
3♣	3NT
No	

2NT = strong enquiry. 3♣ = weak two in hearts, either maximum points or if minimum, the hand includes two top honours in hearts. The heart suit is not strong enough for a jump to 4♡.

Page 75

1.

W	E
2◇	2♡
No	

2♡ = to play opposite a weak two in hearts. If East were sure that West had a weak two, East would want to make some more adventure-some move (such as 3♡ pre-emptive or a 2NT psyche). The trouble with these moves is that if you hit a strong hand with West, you will be killing your own side. Over 2NT you might hear 4NT. Over 3♡, a 3NT rebid will prevent you exploring the possibility of a spade game. The multi-2◇ does not lend itself to psychic responses. Play down the middle and accept the good results which the system itself produces.

2.

W	E
2◇	2NT
3◇	3♡
3♠	No

2NT = strong enquiry. 3◇ = weak two in spades. 3♡ enquires further about the range of the weak two. 3♠ = minimum points, but two top honours in spades. East was interested in game only opposite maximum points. Over 3♡, 3NT would show maximum points and two top honours and 4♣ = maximum points with only one top honour.

3.

W	E
2◇	2NT
3♣	3◇
3♡	3NT
No	

2NT = strong enquiry. 3♣ = goodish weak two in hearts. 3◇ enquires further about the range of the weak two. 3♡ = minimum points but two top honours in hearts. East can now count nine tricks in no-trumps. Had West shown maximum points, but only one top honour in hearts, East would play in 4♡, not 3NT.

4.

W	E
2◇	2NT
3◇	3♡
3NT	4♣
4◇	7♠
No	

2NT = strong enquiry. 3◇ = goodish weak two in spades. 3♡ = further enquiry. 3NT = maximum points and two top honours in spades. 4♣ = cue bid, ♣A, with spades agreed as trumps. 4◇ = cue bid, ◇A. That is enough for East to try 7♠.

5.

W	E
2◇	2NT
3♣	3♠
4♠	No

2NT = strong enquiry. 3♣ = goodish weak two in hearts. 3♠ = natural, genuine spade suit. To set hearts, continue with 3◇ over 3♡, as in above examples.

6. W   E   2NT = strong enquiry. 3♣ = hearts, goodish.
    2◇   2NT   3◇ = Tell me more. 3♠ = Maximum points
    3♣   3◇   and two top honours in hearts. 4♣ = cue bid,
    3♠   4♣   ♣A. 4♡ = no ace to cue. 4♠ = cue bid, ♠A.
    4♡   4♠   5♠ = cue bid, second round control in spades.
    5♠   6♡   That's what East wanted to hear.
    No

7. W   E   3◇ = natural, forcing. 3♡ = weak two in
    2◇   3◇   hearts without support for diamonds. 3NT is a
    3♡   3NT   reasonable gamble, although West could sen-
    No   sibly remove 3NT to 4♡.

8. W   E   3♣ = natural, forcing. 4♠ = weak two in
    2◇   3♣   spades and support for clubs as well. 5♣ = to
    4♠   5♣   play.
    No

9. W   E   Expecting West to hold hearts, East bids 3◇.
    2◇   3◇   3♠ = weak two in spades but no support for
    3♠   4NT   diamonds. Opposite a 6-card spade suit, slam
    5◇   6♠   is likely; East checks on aces and bids 6♠
    No   when West shows one ace.

10. W   E   3◇ = natural, forcing. Opposite a long dia-
    2◇   3◇   mond suit and a good hand, slam is virtually a
    4NT   5♡   certainty from West's point of view. West goes
    5NT   6◇   all the way after finding two aces and a king on
    7NT   No   the basis of the long diamonds.

11. W   E   3◇ = natural, forcing. Again West sees the
    2◇   3◇   slam potential opposite the strongish hand
    4NT   5♡   implied by 3◇. Finding two aces and a king is
    5NT   6◇   enough for West to bid the grand slam.
    7♣   No

12. W   E   With a poor hand, East takes a gamble and
    2◇   3♡   bids 3♡, pre-emptive opposite a weak two in
    3NT   4♡   either major. 3NT shows the 23–24 balanced
    No   hand. East can convert that to 4♡. Had East
                      bid 2♠ initially, East would be able to transfer
    to hearts over West's 2NT rebid. That is the price to pay for East's
    3♡ gamble.

Page 77

1.

W	E
2♦	2NT
3♦	3♡
3♠	4NT
5♡	7NT
No	

2♦ = multi. 2NT = strong enquiry. 3♦ = weak two in spades, goodish; 3♡ = enquiry. 3♠ = minimum points, but two top honours in spades. 4NT asks for key cards, spades set as trumps. 5♡ = 2 key cards, no ♠Q. West has A-K-x-x-x-x in spades therefore, making 7NT a good bet.

2.

W	E
2♦	2NT
3♣	3♦
3♡	4NT
5♦	6♡
No	

2♦ = multi. 2NT = strong enquiry. 3♣ = weak two in hearts, goodish. 3♦ = enquiry. 3♡ = minimum points, but two top honours in hearts. 4NT asks for key cards, hearts set as trumps. 5♦ = one key card only, so 6♡ is the limit. This will be easy on a non-diamond lead and probably down on a diamond lead.

3.

W	E
2♣	2♦
2♡	3♡
4NT	5♣
5♡	No

2♣ = game force. 2♦ = negative. 2♡ = natural. 3♡ = strong raise. 4NT asks for key cards for hearts. 5♣ = 0 or 3, clearly 0 with a negative. 5♡ = sign-off.

4.

W	E
2♣	2♦
2♡	3♡
4NT	5♦
6♡	No

The auction begins as for No. 3. The 5♦ reply to 4NT shows 1 or 4 key cards, clearly one. That is enough for West to bid 6♡. West does not mind whether East has the ♣A or the ♡K. Note that East has the same points in 3 and 4. The right king in 4 gives East–West a slam. The wrong king in 3 means 6♡ would be a poor risk.

5.

W	E
No	2♣
3♣	3♡
4♡	4NT
5♦	6♡
No	

2♣ = game-force. 3♣ = natural, positive. 3♡ = natural. 4♡ = natural. 4NT asks for key cards for hearts. 5♦ = 1 or 4, clearly one. With one key card missing, East settles for the small slam.

6.

W	E
No	2♣
3♣	3♡
4♡	4NT
5♡	7NT
No	

The bidding starts the same as for No. 5. The 5♡ reply shows two key cards but no ♡Q. East knows West has ♡K and ♣A and that is enough to bid 7NT. Note the contrast between 5 and 6. West has the same values, but the right king gives East–West a grand slam.

7. | W | E |
    |---|---|
    | 1♣ | 2♠ |
    | 3♠ | 4NT |
    | 5♡ | 6♠ |
    | No | |

East's 2♠ = powerful, 5+ spades. 3♠ = support. 4NT asks for key cards with spades set as trumps. 5♡ = two key cards but no ♠Q. With only 8–9 trumps and the ♠Q missing, a grand slam would be too risky.

8. | W | E |
    |---|---|
    | 1♣ | 2♠ |
    | 3♠ | 4NT |
    | 5♠ | 7♠ |
    | No | |

The bidding starts as for No. 7. The 5♠ reply shows two key cards plus the ♠Q. That is enough for East to bid 7♠. With a strong trump fit, including the top three trumps and no losers in the first three rounds of any suit, a grand slam is a good bet.

9. | W | E |
    |---|---|
    | 1◇ | 1♠ |
    | 3♠ | 4NT |
    | 5♣ | 5◇ |
    | 5♡ | 6♠ |
    | No | |

After West's jump to 3♠, East naturally looks for a slam. 4NT = Roman Key Card Blackwood. 5♣ = 0 to 3 key cards, clearly three because of West's strong bid. 5◇ = 'Do you have the queen of trumps?' 5♡ = No. That ends East's hopes for a grand slam.

10. | W | E |
    |---|---|
    | 1◇ | 1♠ |
    | 3♠ | 4NT |
    | 5♣ | 5◇ |
    | 5♠ | 7♠ |
    | No | |

The bidding starts the same way as No. 9. Over 5♣, 5◇ asks for the trump queen. 5♠, up two steps, says, 'I have the trump queen.' East can now bid the grand slam. If worried, East could bid 5NT asking for kings outside trumps. West bids 6◇ showing one such king.

11. | W | E |
    |---|---|
    | 1♣ | 1♡ |
    | 3♡ | 4NT |
    | 5◇ | 5♡ |
    | No | |

5◇ over 4NT shows 1 or 4 key cards. East is unsure which it is. Always assume the worst. East signs off and with only one key card, West must pass.

12. | W | E |
    |---|---|
    | 1♣ | 1♡ |
    | 3♡ | 4NT |
    | 5◇ | 5♡ |
    | 5♠ | 6♡ |
    | No | |

Where the reply to 4NT RKCB is ambiguous and partner signs off, you always bid on if you hold the higher number of key cards. 5◇ = 1 or 4 key cards. 5♡ = sign-off if it is only one key card. 5♠ = it is four key cards, but I do not have the ♡Q. East settles for 6♡. If West had the ♡Q as well (a bit too much for the 3♡ rebid, perhaps), West would bid 5NT over 5♡, saying 'I have the four key cards and the ♡Q as well.' East would then bid 7♡.

Page 79

1. | W | E |
    |---|---|
    | 3♣ | 4◇ |
    | 4♠ | 5♣ |
    | No | |

    Over 3♣, 4◇ sets clubs and asks for key cards. 4♠ shows 1 or 4 key cards (obviously only one for a pre-emptor). With two key cards missing, East signs off in 5♣.

2. | W | E |
    |---|---|
    | 3♣ | 4◇ |
    | 4NT | 6NT |
    | No | |

    The 4NT reply to the 4◇ key card ask shows two key cards but no ♣Q. That is enough for East to bid the small slam and at pairs, it is best to bid the slam in no-trumps.

3. | W | E |
    |---|---|
    | 3♠ | 4♣ |
    | 4◇ | 4♠ |
    | No | |

    Over 3◇, 3♡ or 3♠, the key card ask is 4♣. West's 4◇ shows 0 or 3 key cards. It must be 0 for a pre-emptor. Note that 4NT by East would lead to 5♠, one off.

4. | W | E |
    |---|---|
    | 3♠ | 4♣ |
    | 4♡ | 4♠ |
    | No | |

    This time West bids 4♡ showing one key card. Again this is not enough for East to bid beyond game.

5. | W | E |
    |---|---|
    | 3♠ | 4♣ |
    | 4♠ | 6♠ |
    | No | |

    Here West's 4♠ reply shows two key cards, but no ♠Q. Two key cards is what East was hoping for. 6♠ is likely to be a good slam.

6. | W | E |
    |---|---|
    | 3♠ | 4NT |
    | 5◇ | 6♡ |
    | No | |

    As 4♣ is a key card ask with spades as trumps, 4NT is simple Blackwood for aces. Opener intends to play in his own suit or in no-trumps. 5◇ = one ace. 6♡ = to play.

7. | W | E |
    |---|---|
    | 3♠ | 4NT |
    | 5♣ | 5♡ |
    | No | |

    4NT = simple Blackwood as in No. 6. 5♣ = no aces. 5♡ = to play.

8. | W | E |
    |---|---|
    | 4◇ | 4NT |
    | 5♠ | 6♠ |
    | No | |

    The 4◇ opening is a strong pre-empt of 4♠. 4NT sets spades and asks for key cards. 5♠ shows two key cards and the ♠Q. That makes 6♠ a good bet from East's point of view.

9.
W	E
4NT	6♣
No	

4NT = a 5-level minor suit pre-empt with a suit headed by the A-K-Q. 6♣ is to play if the suit is clubs (which East knows). Note that 6♣ by East is excellent.

10.
W	E
5♣	No

The 5♣ opening indicates at least one top honour in clubs is missing (failure to open 4NT). East therefore has no slam ambitions.

11.
W	E
3◇	3♠
4♠	4NT
5◇	5♡
5NT	7NT
No	

3♠ = natural, forcing. 4♠ = support. 4NT asks for key cards based on spades. 5◇ shows one key card (East knows it is the ◇A). 5♡ asks for the trump queen. 5NT = Yes, I have the ♠Q. East might now bid 7♠ or take a shot at 7NT. 7♠ is safer but 7NT, counting on five club winners is certainly reasonable at pairs.

12.
W	E
4♣	4NT
5♠	7NT
No	

4♣ = strong 4♡ pre-empt. It should contain eight playing tricks. 4NT asks for key cards based on hearts. 5♠ = two key cards plus the ♡Q. East knows that is A-K-Q in hearts. If West has eight playing tricks in hearts, East can supply five more. Hence, 7NT.

Page 81

1.
W	N	E	S
No	1♡	Dbl	No
2♣	No	2♠	No
No	No		

East is too strong for an overcall. The double-then-new-suit shows a 5+ card suit and 15–18 points, about a 5–6 loser hand.

2.
W	N	E	S
No	1◇	2♠	No
4♠	No	No	No

2♠ = weak jump-overcall, 6–10 points. With a 10-card fit, West should bid game, either to make or as a sacrifice.

3.

W	N	E	S
	1♣	Dbl	No
No	1♣	Dbl	No
1♠	No	3♡	No
4♡	No	No	No

East is too strong for an overcall. The way to show a 4-loser hand after an opponent opens is to double and jump on the next round. East's 3♡ indicates a strong heart suit and nine playing tricks (four losers). With a sure winner, partner is expected to bid on and that is just what West does.

4.

W	N	E	S
			1♡
2♣	No	3NT	No
No	No		

2♣ = natural overcall. With 15 points, hearts well stopped and a fit with the clubs, East has more than enough to try 3NT.

5.

W	N	E	S
No	1♡	1♠	No
3♠	No	No	No

1♠ = normal overcall. 3♠ = pre-emptive raise, 4+ trumps and about 8 losers. Little defence in the outside suits.

6.

W	N	E	S
No	1♡	1NT	No
2♣	No	2♠	No
4♠	No	No	No

1NT = 16–18 points, 2♣ = Stayman, 2♠ = four spades.

7.

W	N	E	S
No	1♣	1♠	No
1NT	No	2◇	No
No	No		

1♠ = normal overcall. 1NT = no support for spades, about 7–10 points and clubs stopped. East might pass 1NT, but most would prefer 2◇ with an unbalanced hand.

8.

W	N	E	S
			1◇
1♡	No	2◇	No
3♣	No	3♡	No
4♡	No	No	No

1♡ = normal overcall. 2◇ = strong hand asking West to clarify the overcall. 3♣ = genuine second suit. 3♡ = support for hearts and is an invite to game since it was preceded by the 2◇ bid.

Page 83

1.

W	N	E	S
	1◇	Dbl	2◇
Dbl	No	2♠	No
No	No		

East has a routine takeout double. West's double is responsive showing equal length in the majors. That allows East to pick the major and the better trump fit is found.

2.

W	N	E	S
			1♡
Dbl	2♡	Dbl	No
3◇	No	No	No

West has a standard takeout double. East's double is responsive, showing equal length in the minors, enabling the partnership to find the better minor fit.

3.

W	N	E	S
			1♡
Dbl	2♡	2♠	No
No	No		

If they bid and raise hearts, do not use a responsive double if you have spades. Simply bid the spades.

4.

W	N	E	S
	1♡	Dbl	3♡
Dbl	No	4♣	No
No	No		

The responsive double can be used also after a raise to the 3-level. West's double shows both minors and enough to justify competing to the 4-level. East bids the better minor.

5.

W	N	E	S
1♡	No	1♠	2◇
No	No	Dbl	No
3♣	No	No	No

Over 2◇, West is too weak to bid 3♣ (16+ points would be implied). When 2◇ is passed to East, a 3♣ bid would be forcing. East is not strong enough for that.

As long as East–West use takeout doubles at the 1-level and 2-level, this is easy. East doubles for takeout and West bids 3♣. Thus East–West find their best fit without overbidding their cards.

6.

W	N	E	S
1♣	No	1♠	2◇
Dbl	No	2♠	No
No	No		

West's double is competitive, not penalties. It shows a shortage in diamonds and denies four spades. East rebids the spades, showing only 6–9 points and five spades.

As West is minimum, West passes 2♠.

7.

W	N	E	S
		1◇	No
1♡	2♣	No	No
Dbl	No	2♠	No
No	No		

East has no sound action over 2♣. Rather than sell out to 2♣, West doubles for takeout (competitive double). West can stand 2◇, 2♡ or 2♠ from East. East naturally bids 2♠. West has no reason to bid on. You should note how these takeout doubles at the two-level find the right spot easily. How would East–West cope without doubling?

8.

W	N	E	S
		1♡	No
1♠	2◇	No	No
Dbl	No	No	No

East would like to double 2◇ for penalties (strong trumps, short in partner's suit are the ideal conditions for penalties). However, if you play competitive doubles, double by East would be takeout. East must pass for penalties. West is too weak to bid 3♣, forcing, but can afford a takeout double. This is a common scenario and East passes for penalties.

Page 85

1.

W	N	E	S
	1♠	No	2♠
No	No	2NT	No
3♣	No	No	No

Neither East nor West is worth immediate action. When 2♠ is passed by North, East should not let them play at the two-level after a bid and raise. The delayed 2NT is a takeout for the minors and West naturally bids 3♣.

2.

W	N	E	S
			1♡
No	2♡	No	No
Dbl	No	3♣	No
3◇	No	No	No

East and West are not worth any action on the first round. When 2♡ is about to be passed out, West should compete. The advantage of doubling is that it caters for a spade fit.

3.

W	N	E	S
	1♡	2NT	3♡
5◇	...		

East's 2NT shows both minors, at least 5–5 and about 8–12 points. With a good fit for one minor and no reasonable defence against their game. West takes a sacrifice in 5◇. North–South will either double 5◇ or bid on to 5♡. If they do bid 5♡, East–West should pass.

4.	W	N	E	S
				1♠
	No	2♣	No	No
	Dbl	No	2NT	No
	3◇	No	No	No

West is too weak to double 1♠, although there are some who would. When 2♣ comes back to West, now is the time to double. The delayed double will not mislead partner as to your strength.

East's 2NT shows the minors. In a delayed double auction, it is better to use 2NT as a choice of minors rather than natural. This allows East–West to find their better minor fit.

5.	W	N	E	S
				1♠
	2♠	No	3♣	No
	3◇	No	No	No

2♠ = Michaels Cue Bid, showing a weak 5–5, hearts and a minor. With a weak hand and no heart fit, East bids 3♣. This is corrected by West when diamonds is the other suit.

6.	W	N	E	S
		1♡	2♡	No
	2NT	No	3♣	No
	No	No		

2♡ = Michaels, a weak 5–5, spades and a minor. 2NT is a strong reply. 3♣ shows the second suit and also a minimum hand. Opposite a minimum, West should bid no further.

7.	W	N	E	S
		1♡	2♡	3♡
	4♠	No	No	No

2♡ = Michaels, as above. With a superb fit, West should bid game, either to make or as a sacrifice against their likely 4♡ contract.

8.	W	N	E	S
				1♡
	Dbl	No	2◇	No
	2♡	No	3♣	No
	4NT	No	5♣	No
	No	No		

As 2♡ would be Michaels, the huge hands start with a double. After partner's reply, you then cue-bid their suit to show the powerhouse. When the club fit is revealed, West tries 4NT on the off chance that East might have

the ♡A. 5♣ = no ace and West settles for that.